THAT WAS MY NAME

Written & Illustrated
by

Magdi Menassa Malky

Edited & Revised
by
Lily Magdi Malky

Technical Supervision & Art Revision

by
Colette Ghassan

© Copyright
All rights strictly reserved for writer
First Edition 2011
ISBN : 978-9953-0-2176-8
Lebanese Ministry of Economy
Patent No 4839 reg. date 11 Aug. 2011

Printed in Chemaly & Chemaly Printing Press

In Memory
of

Maryann Hanna Karam

Who Shared in
The Researches of This Book

A SERIES OF STORIES
ABOUT SIMON PETER
A FOLLOWER OF JESUS CHRIST.

THE SERIES IS TAKEN
FROM THE GOSPEL,
AND DECORATED BY THE
AUTHOR'S IMAGINATION.
IN EACH STORY
NEW CHARACTERS APPEAR,
SOME ARE MENTIONED
IN THE BIBLE, SOME ARE NOT.

THE MAP of THE HOLY LAND
IN 30 A.D.

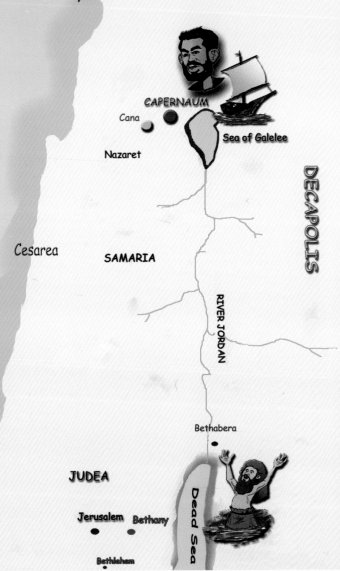

Tyre

CAPERNAUM

Cana

Sea of Galelee

Nazaret

DECAPOLIS

Cesarea

SAMARIA

RIVER JORDAN

Bethabera

JUDEA

Jerusalem   Bethany

Dead Sea

Bethlehem

Stories of Simon

That Was My Name

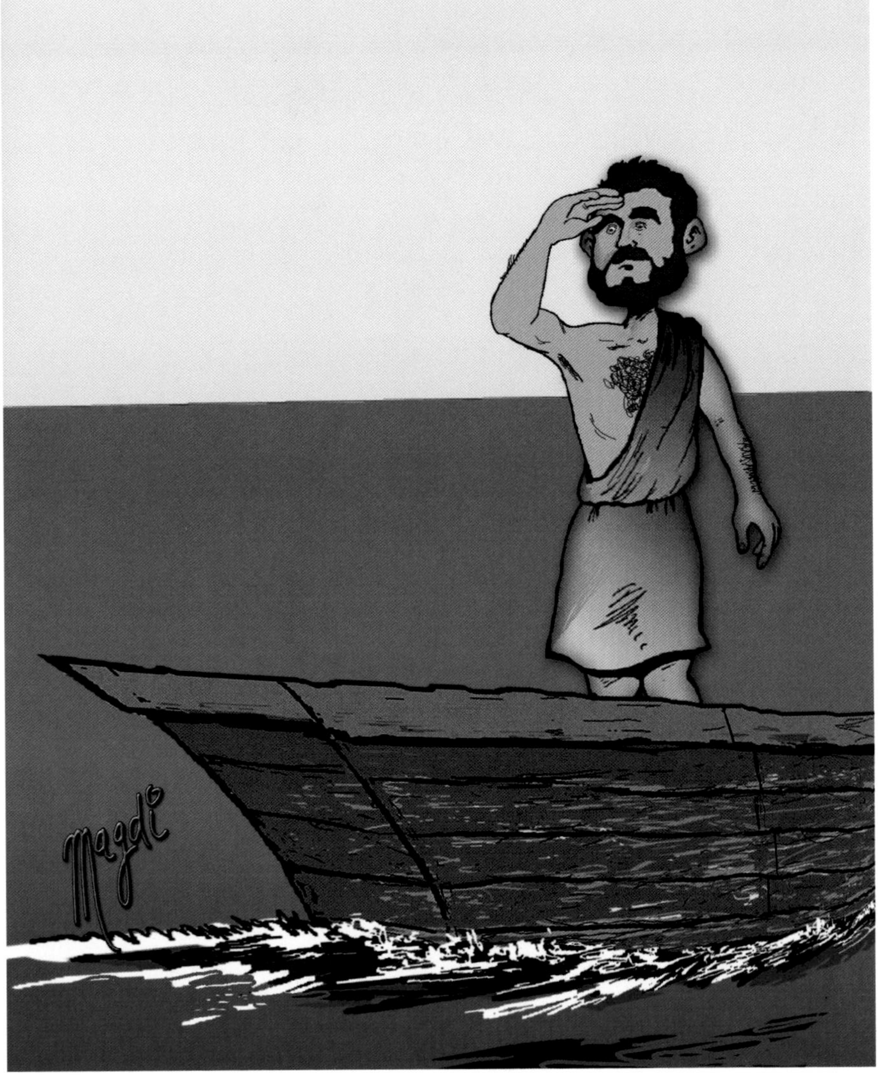
Magdi

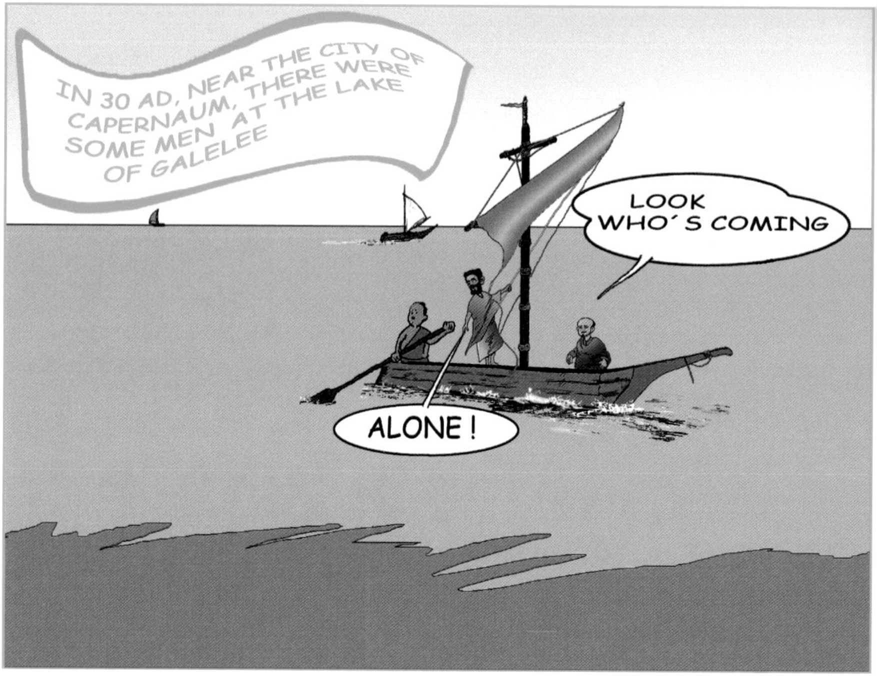
IN 30 AD, NEAR THE CITY OF CAPERNAUM, THERE WERE SOME MEN AT THE LAKE OF GALELEE
LOOK WHO´S COMING
ALONE !

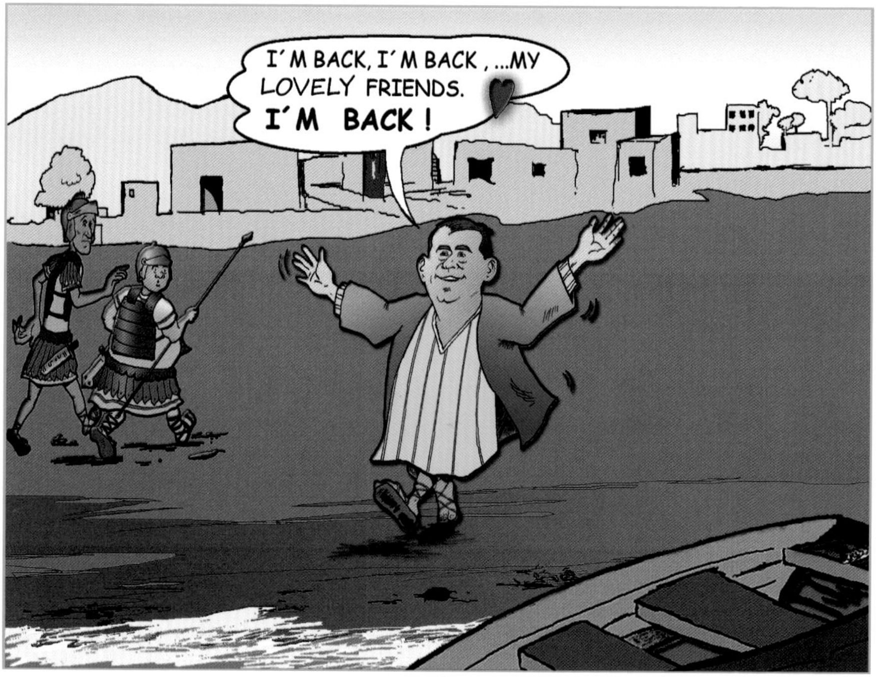
I´M BACK, I´M BACK , ...MY LOVELY FRIENDS. I´M BACK !

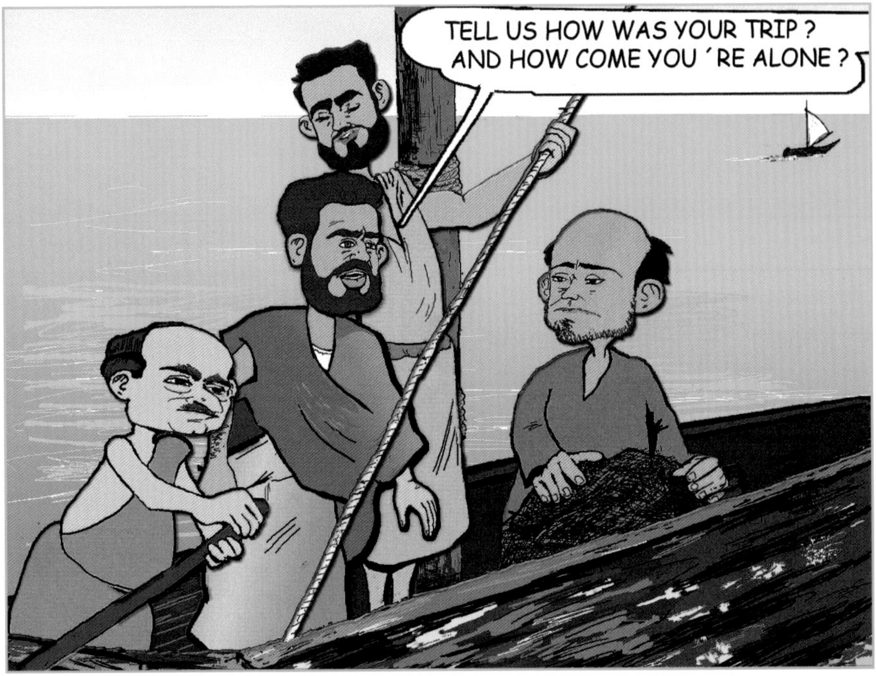
TELL US HOW WAS YOUR TRIP ?
AND HOW COME YOU ´RE ALONE ?

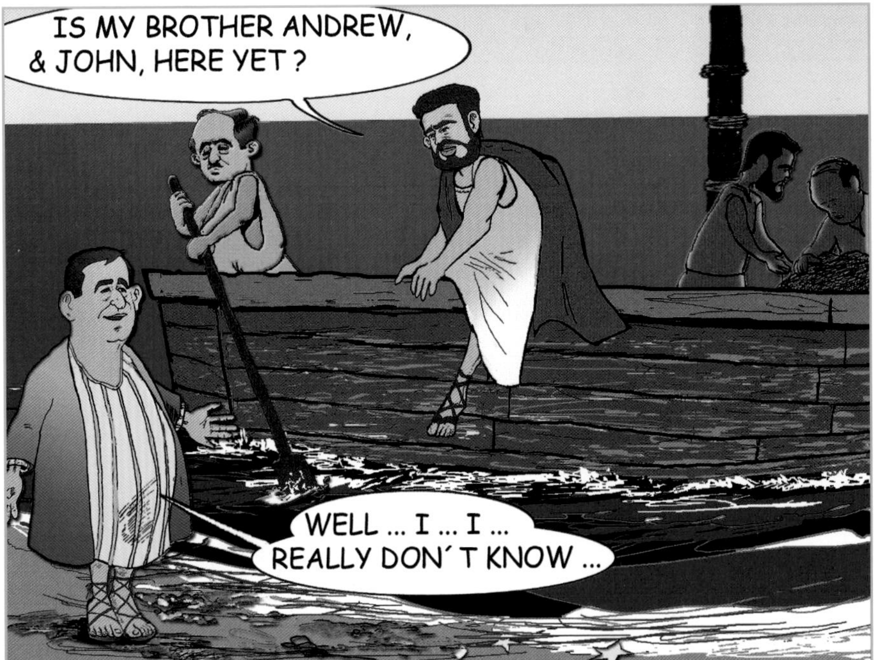
IS MY BROTHER ANDREW,
& JOHN, HERE YET ?
WELL ... I ... I ...
REALLY DON´ T KNOW ...

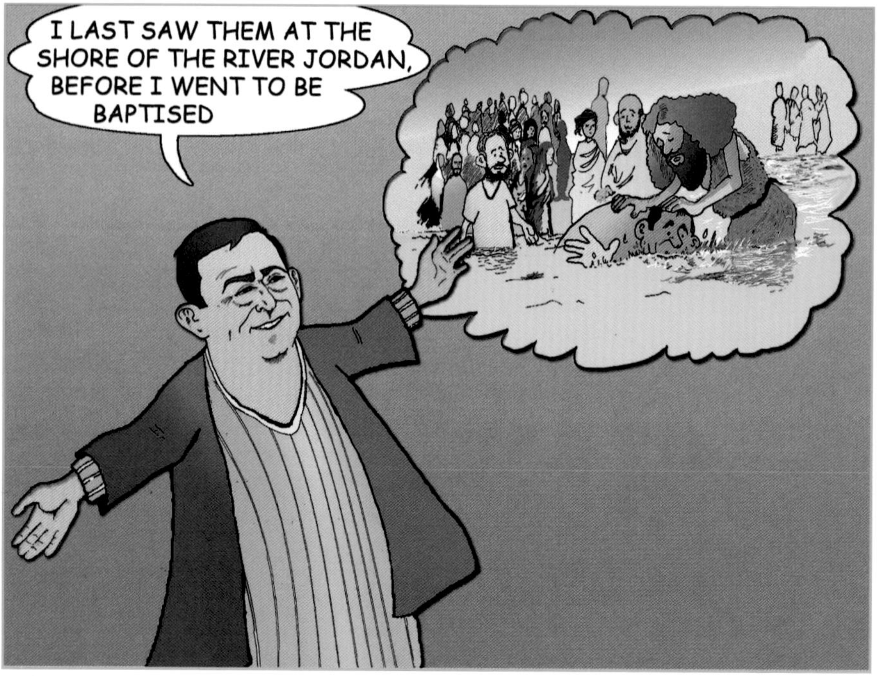
I LAST SAW THEM AT THE SHORE OF THE RIVER JORDAN, BEFORE I WENT TO BE BAPTISED

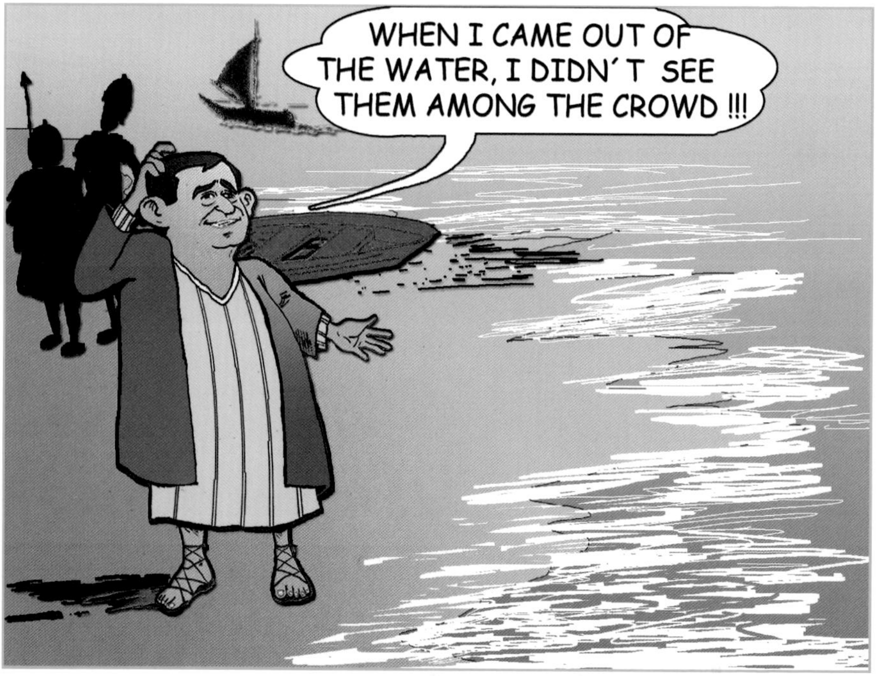
WHEN I CAME OUT OF THE WATER, I DIDN´T SEE THEM AMONG THE CROWD !!!

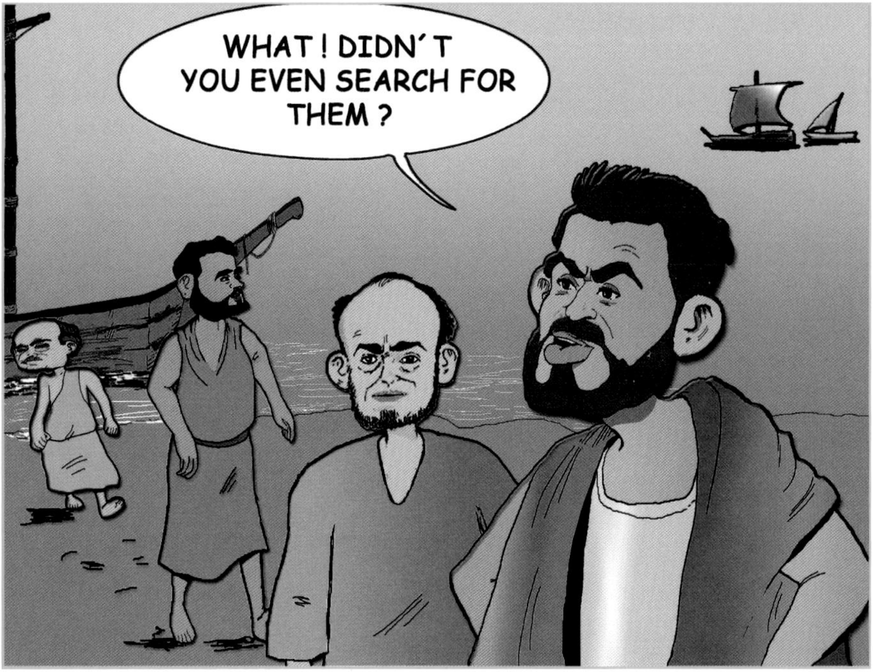
WHAT ! DIDN´T YOU EVEN SEARCH FOR THEM ?

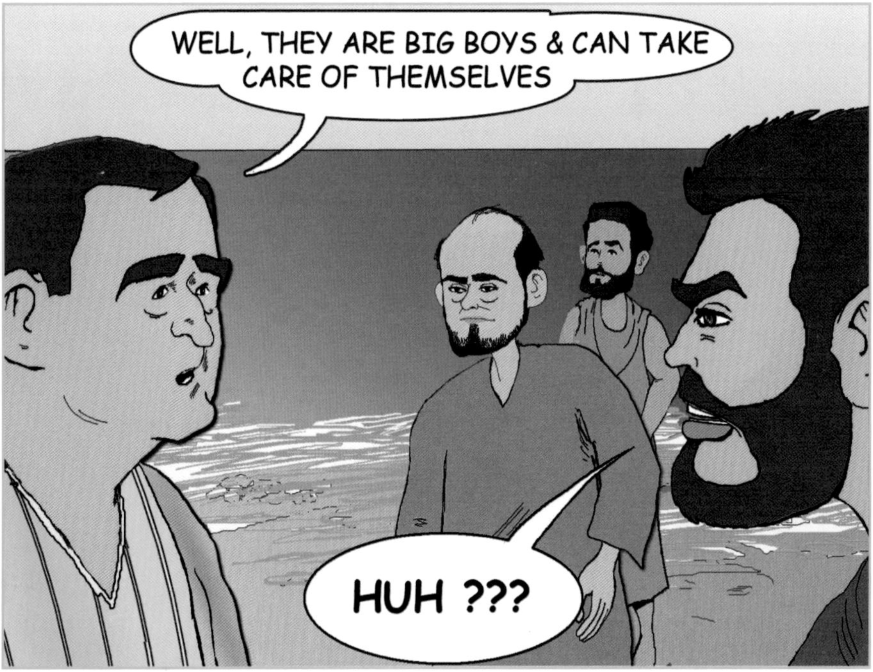
WELL, THEY ARE BIG BOYS & CAN TAKE CARE OF THEMSELVES
HUH ???

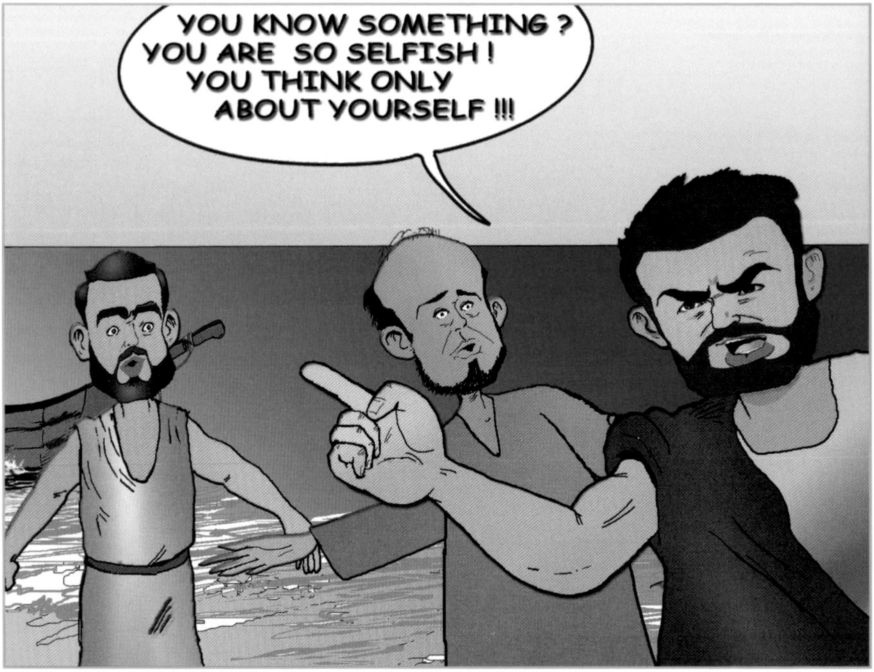
YOU KNOW SOMETHING ? YOU ARE SO SELFISH ! YOU THINK ONLY ABOUT YOURSELF !!!

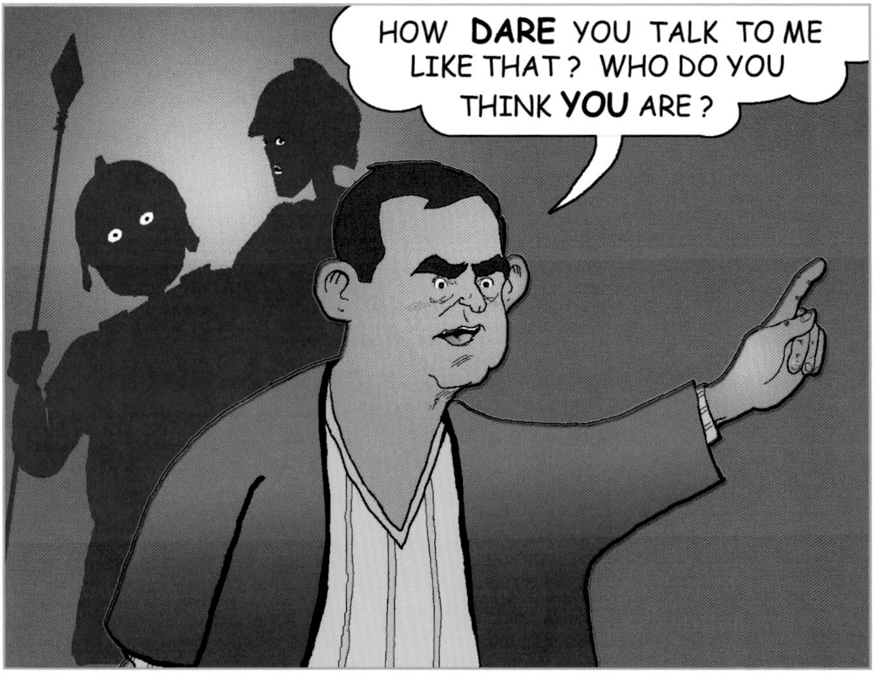
HOW DARE YOU TALK TO ME LIKE THAT ? WHO DO YOU THINK YOU ARE ?

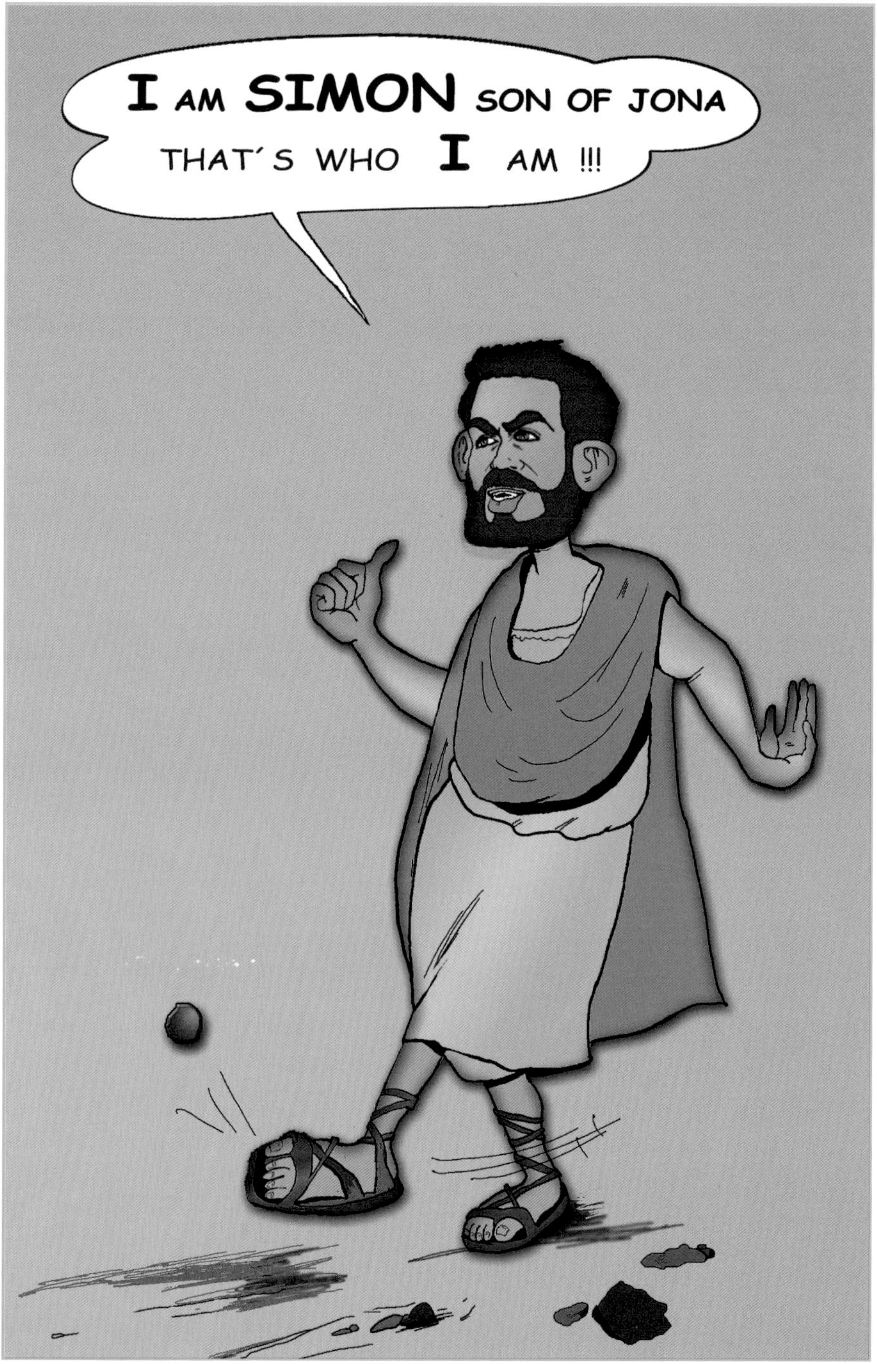
I AM SIMON SON OF JONA
THAT´S WHO I AM !!!

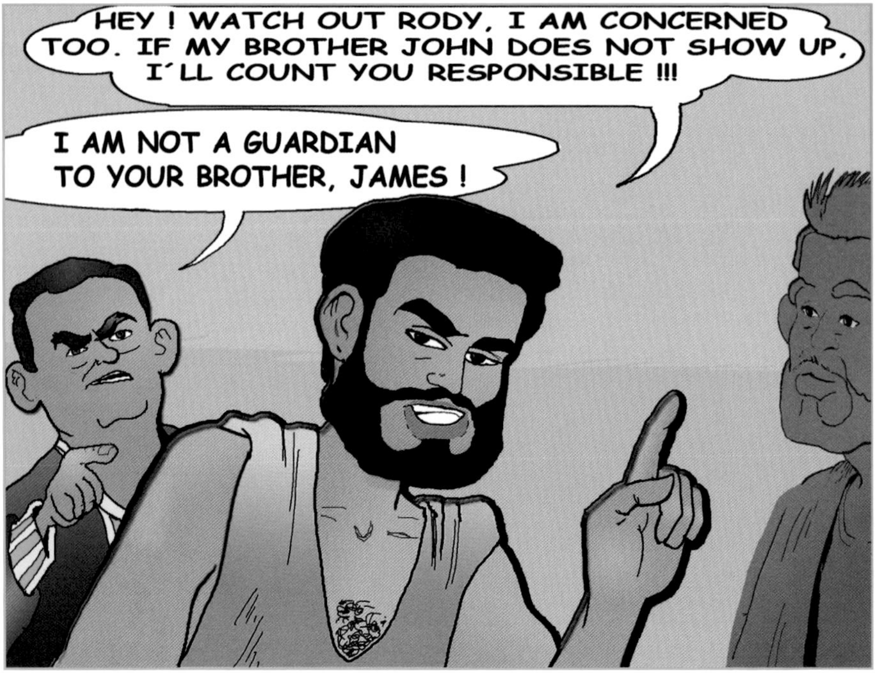
HEY ! WATCH OUT RODY, I AM CONCERNED TOO. IF MY BROTHER JOHN DOES NOT SHOW UP, I´LL COUNT YOU RESPONSIBLE !!!
I AM NOT A GUARDIAN TO YOUR BROTHER, JAMES !

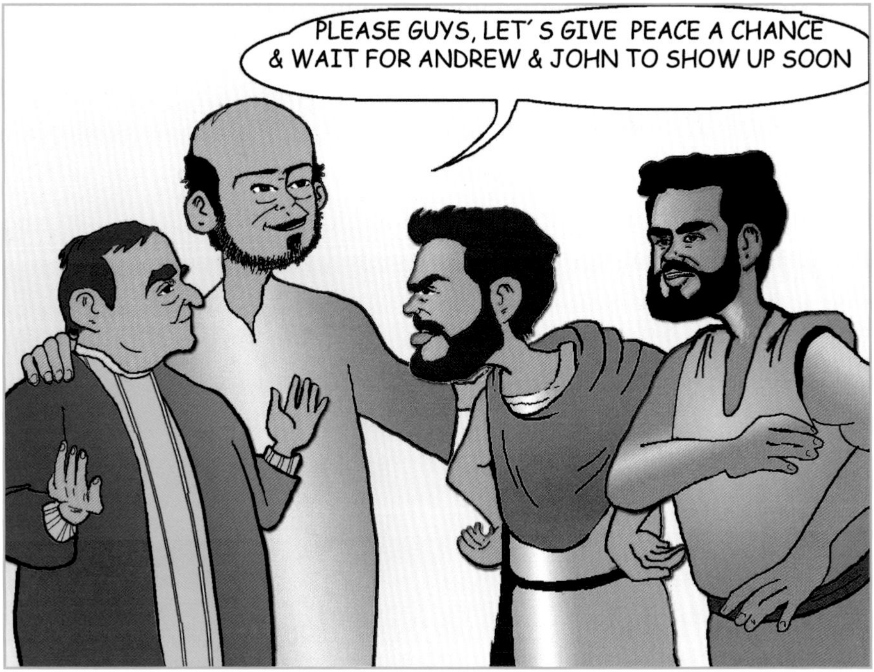
PLEASE GUYS, LET´ S GIVE PEACE A CHANCE & WAIT FOR ANDREW & JOHN TO SHOW UP SOON

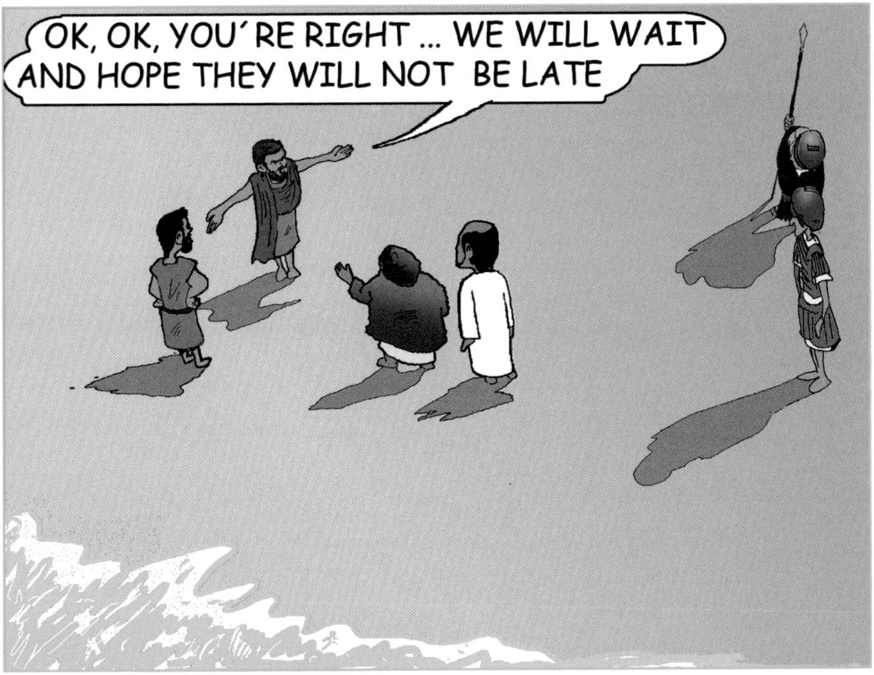
OK, OK, YOU´RE RIGHT ... WE WILL WAIT AND HOPE THEY WILL NOT BE LATE

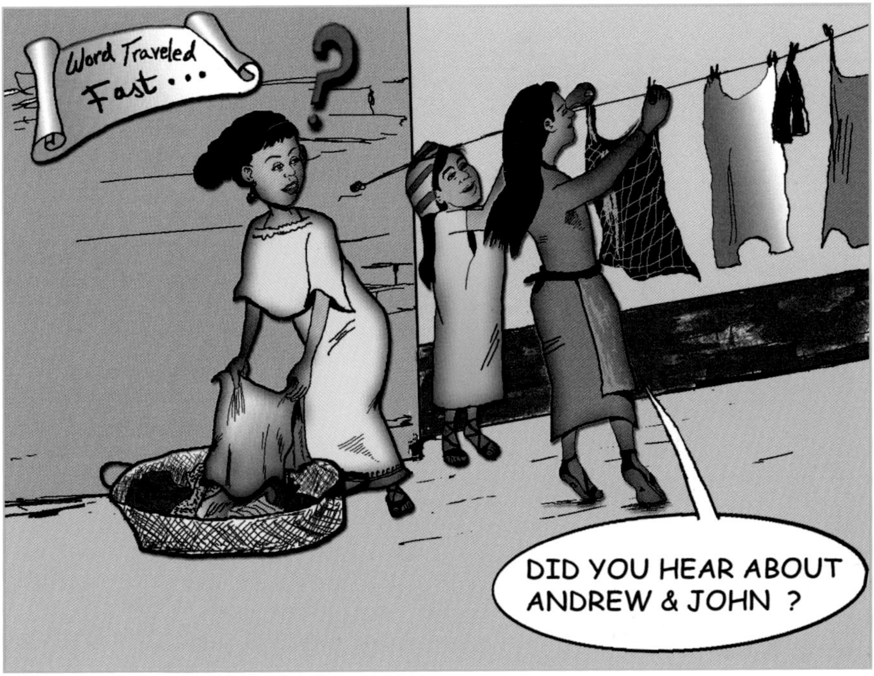
Word Traveled Fast ...
DID YOU HEAR ABOUT ANDREW & JOHN ?

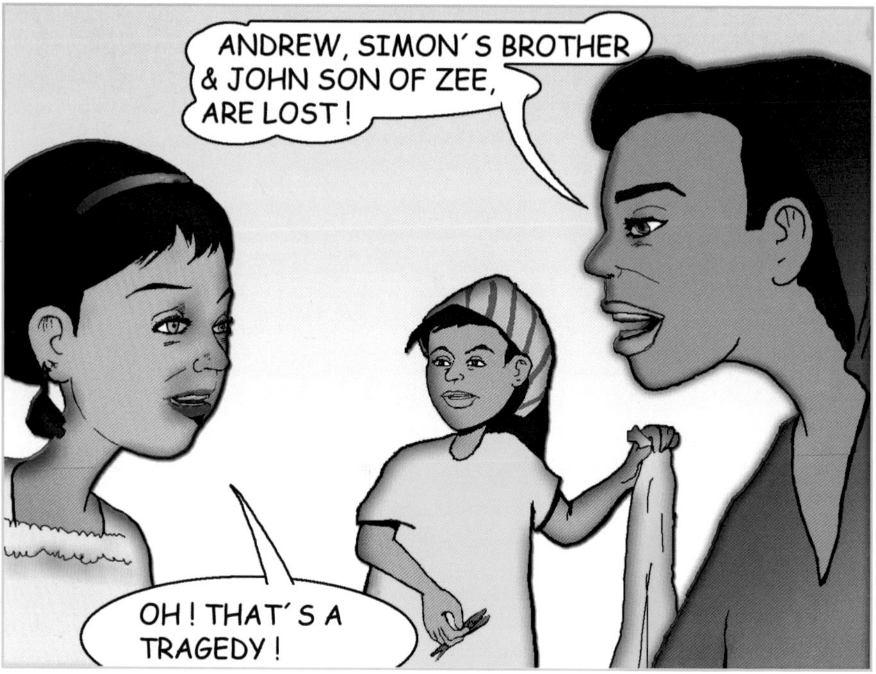
ANDREW, SIMON´S BROTHER & JOHN SON OF ZEE, ARE LOST !
OH ! THAT´S A TRAGEDY !

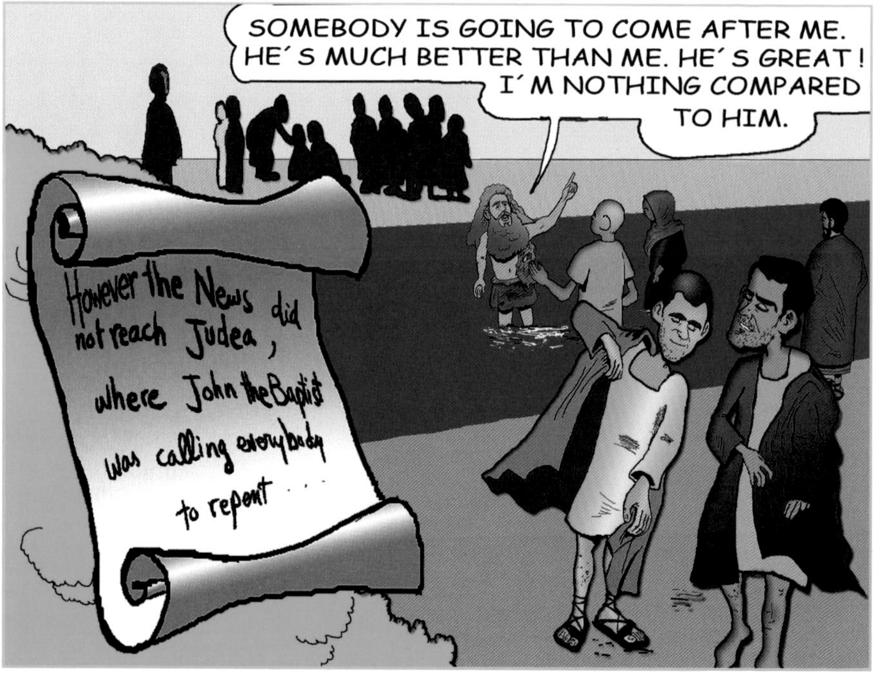
However the News did not reach Judea, where John the Baptist was calling everybody to repent . . .
SOMEBODY IS GOING TO COME AFTER ME. HE´S MUCH BETTER THAN ME. HE´S GREAT ! I´M NOTHING COMPARED TO HIM.

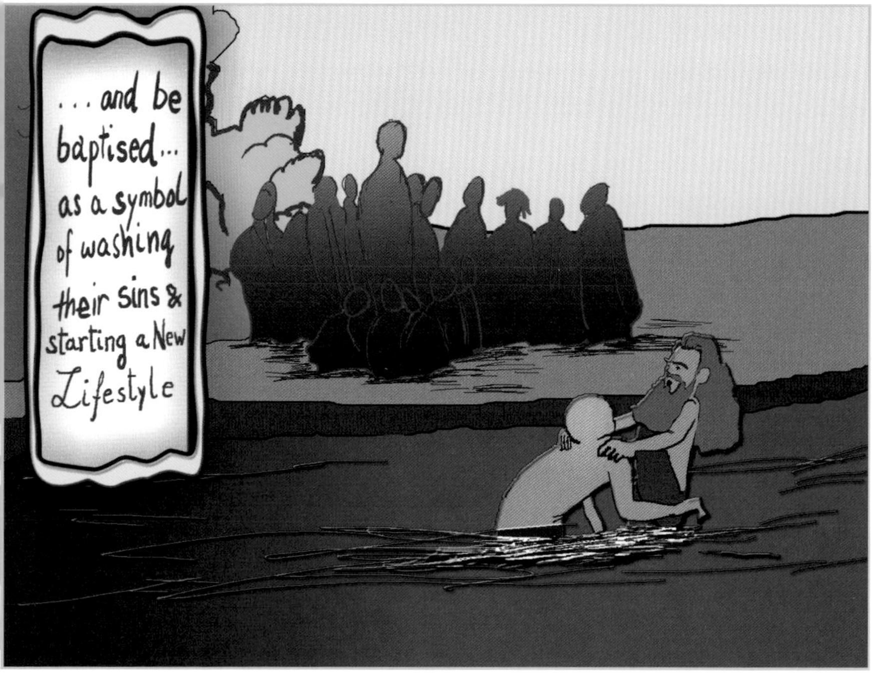
. . . and be baptised... as a symbol of washing their sins & starting a New Lifestyle

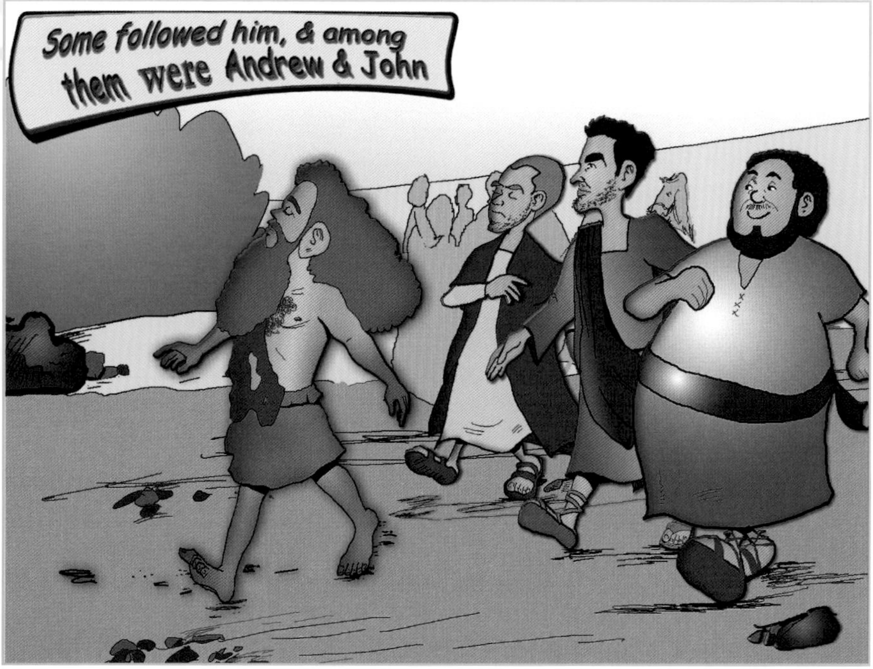
Some followed him, & among them were Andrew & John

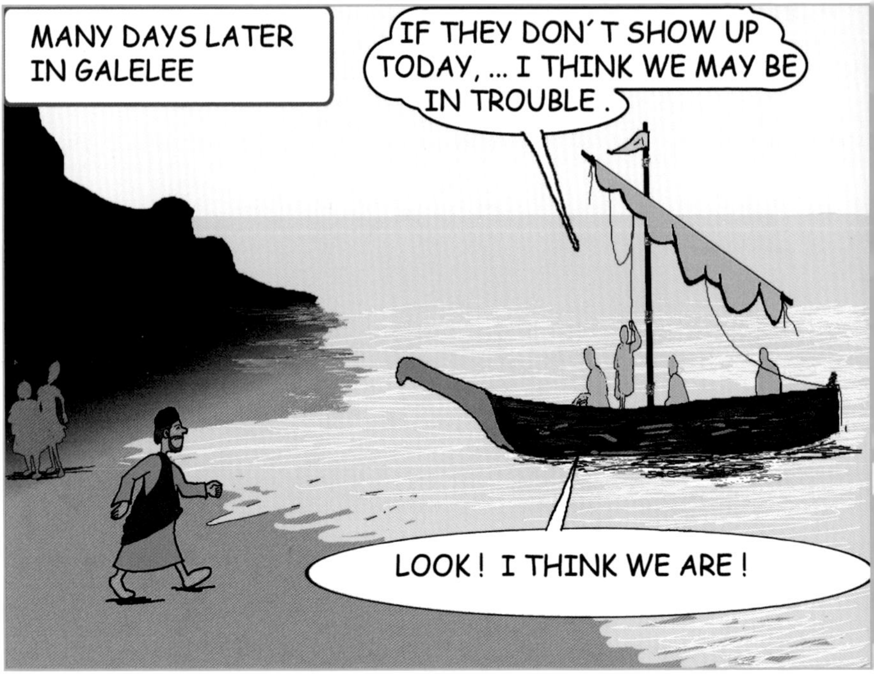
MANY DAYS LATER
IN GALELEE
IF THEY DON´T SHOW UP TODAY, ... I THINK WE MAY BE IN TROUBLE .
LOOK ! I THINK WE ARE !

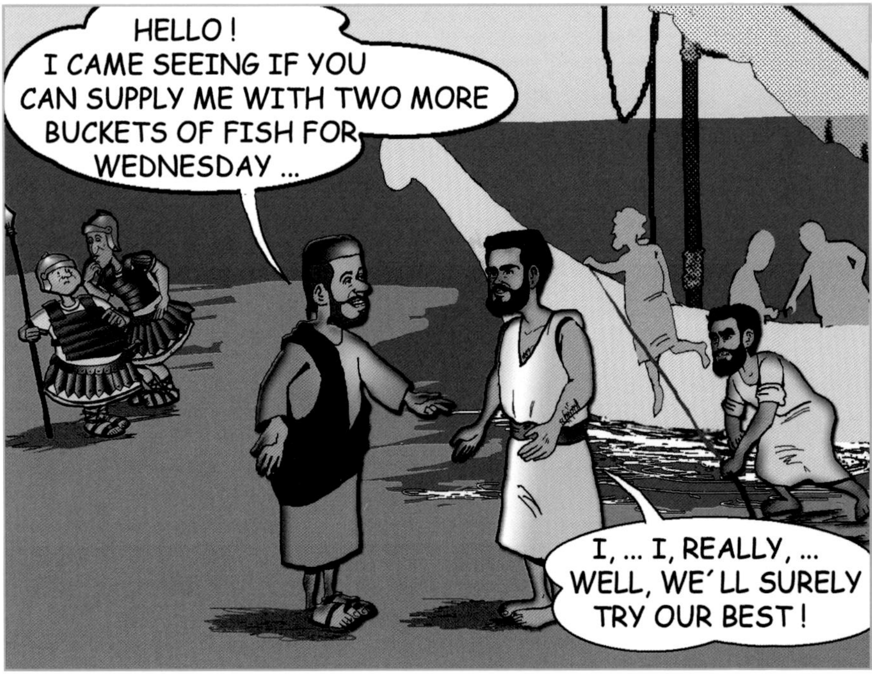
HELLO !
I CAME SEEING IF YOU CAN SUPPLY ME WITH TWO MORE BUCKETS OF FISH FOR WEDNESDAY ...
I, ... I, REALLY, ... WELL, WE´LL SURELY TRY OUR BEST !

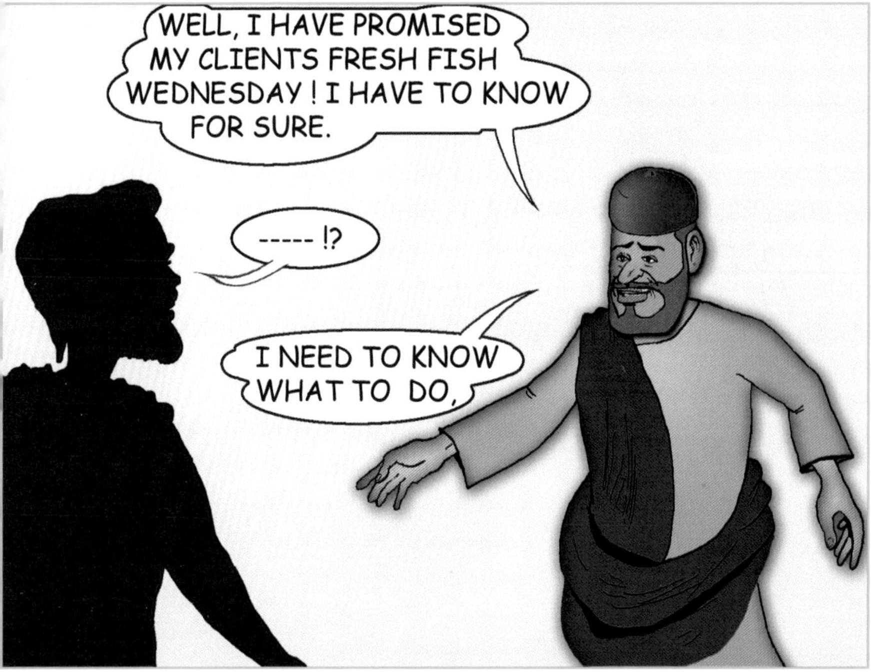
WELL, I HAVE PROMISED MY CLIENTS FRESH FISH WEDNESDAY ! I HAVE TO KNOW FOR SURE.
----- !?
I NEED TO KNOW WHAT TO DO,

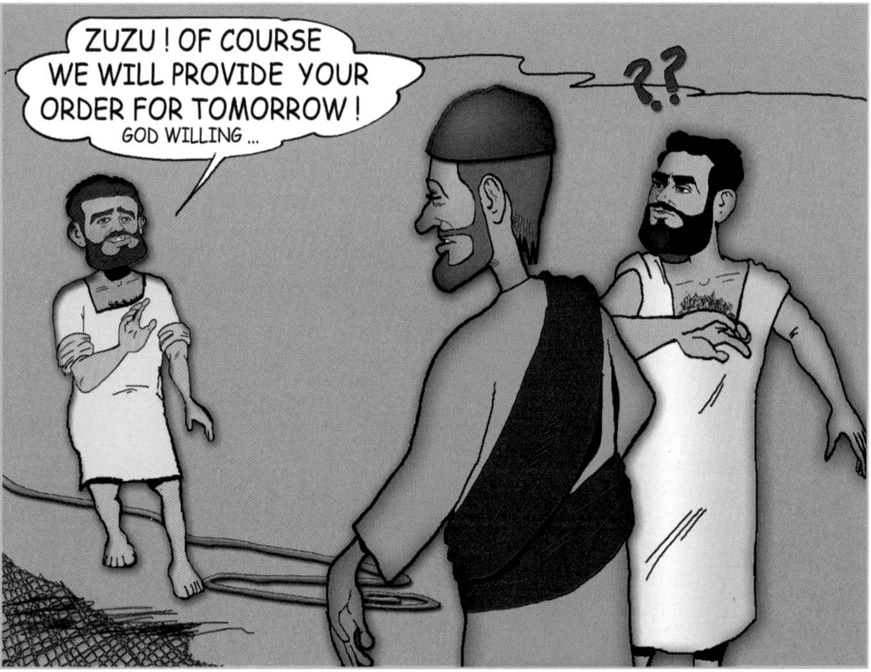
ZUZU ! OF COURSE WE WILL PROVIDE YOUR ORDER FOR TOMORROW ! GOD WILLING ...
??

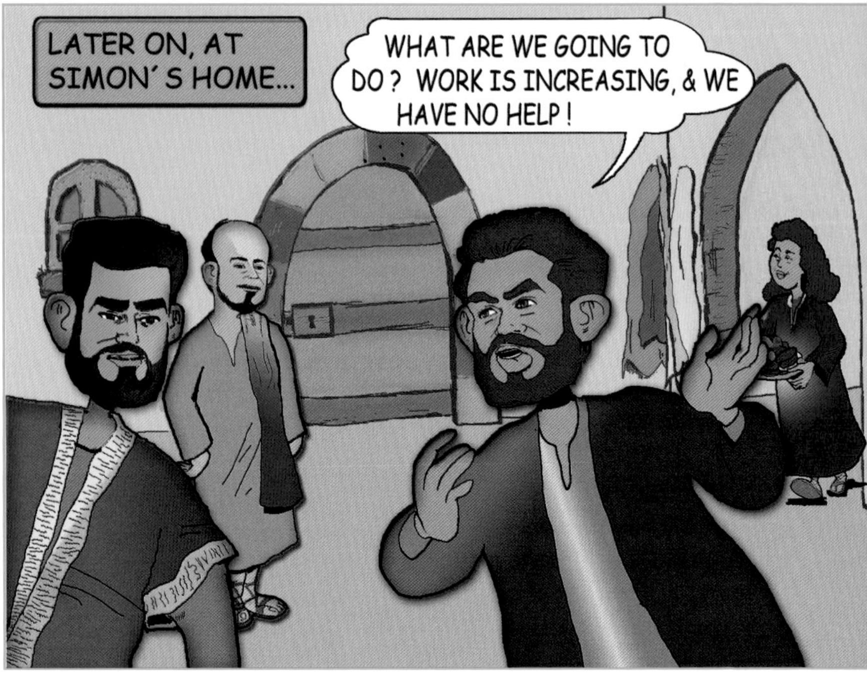
LATER ON, AT SIMON´S HOME...
WHAT ARE WE GOING TO DO ? WORK IS INCREASING, & WE HAVE NO HELP !

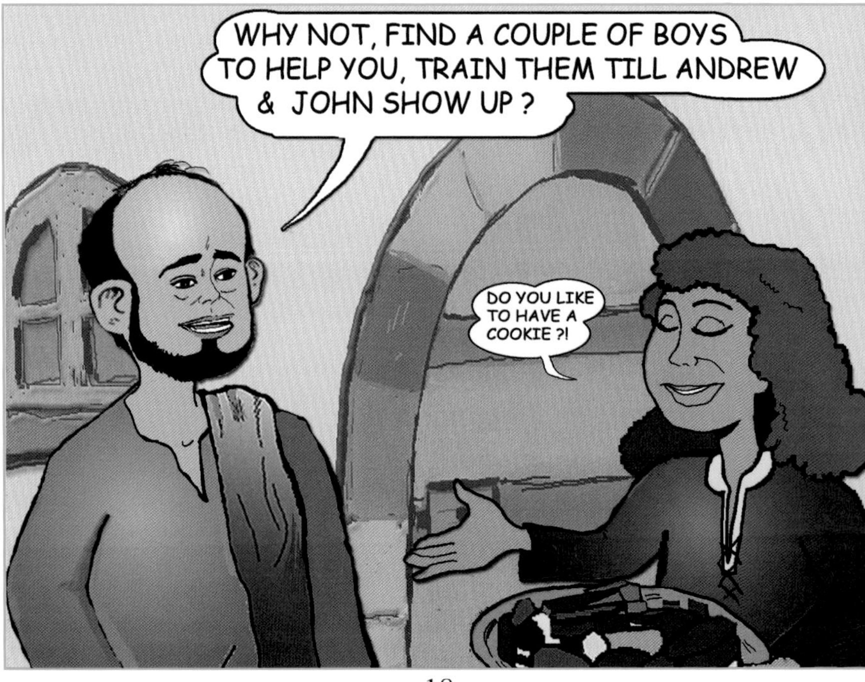
WHY NOT, FIND A COUPLE OF BOYS TO HELP YOU, TRAIN THEM TILL ANDREW & JOHN SHOW UP ?
DO YOU LIKE TO HAVE A COOKIE ?!

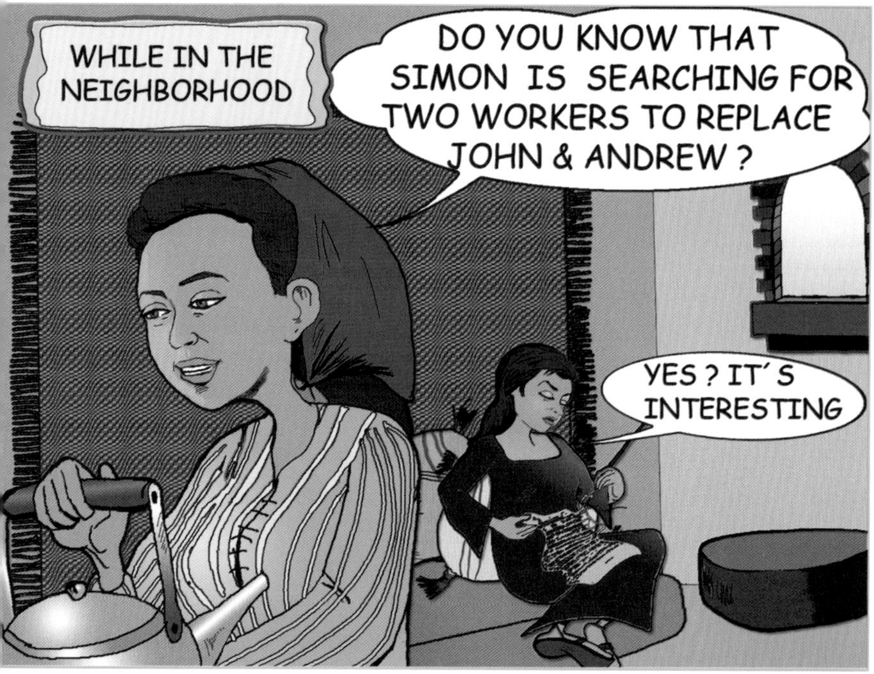
WHILE IN THE NEIGHBORHOOD
DO YOU KNOW THAT SIMON IS SEARCHING FOR TWO WORKERS TO REPLACE JOHN & ANDREW ?
YES ? IT´S INTERESTING

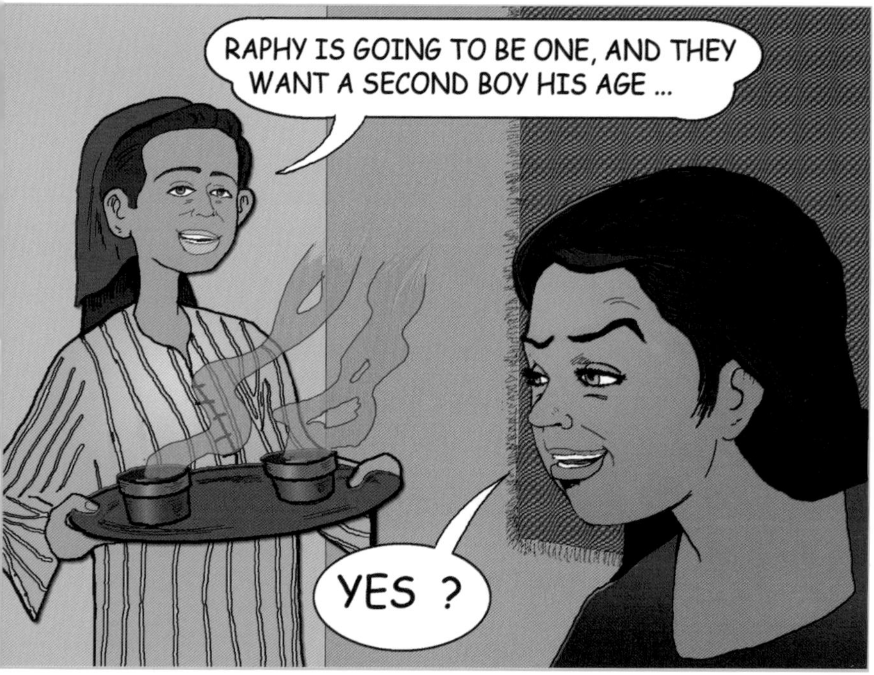
RAPHY IS GOING TO BE ONE, AND THEY WANT A SECOND BOY HIS AGE ...
YES ?

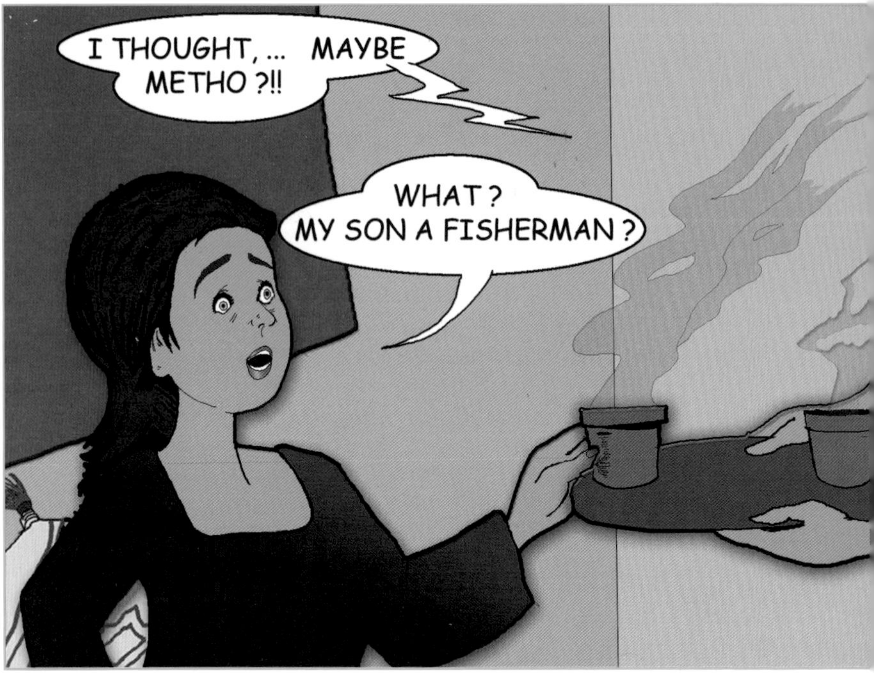
I THOUGHT, ... MAYBE METHO ?!!
WHAT ? MY SON A FISHERMAN ?

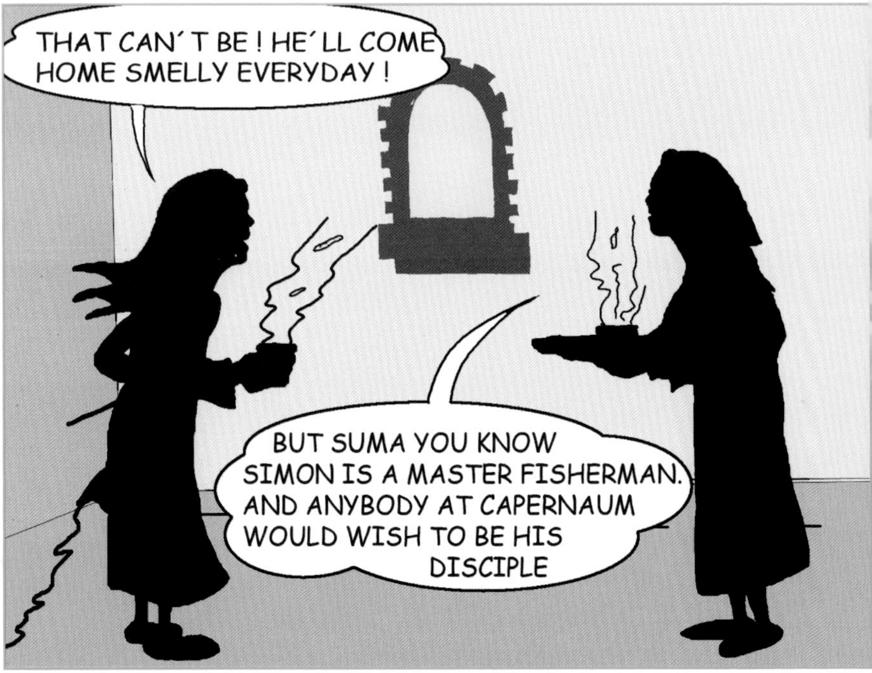
THAT CAN´T BE ! HE´LL COME HOME SMELLY EVERYDAY !
BUT SUMA YOU KNOW SIMON IS A MASTER FISHERMAN. AND ANYBODY AT CAPERNAUM WOULD WISH TO BE HIS DISCIPLE

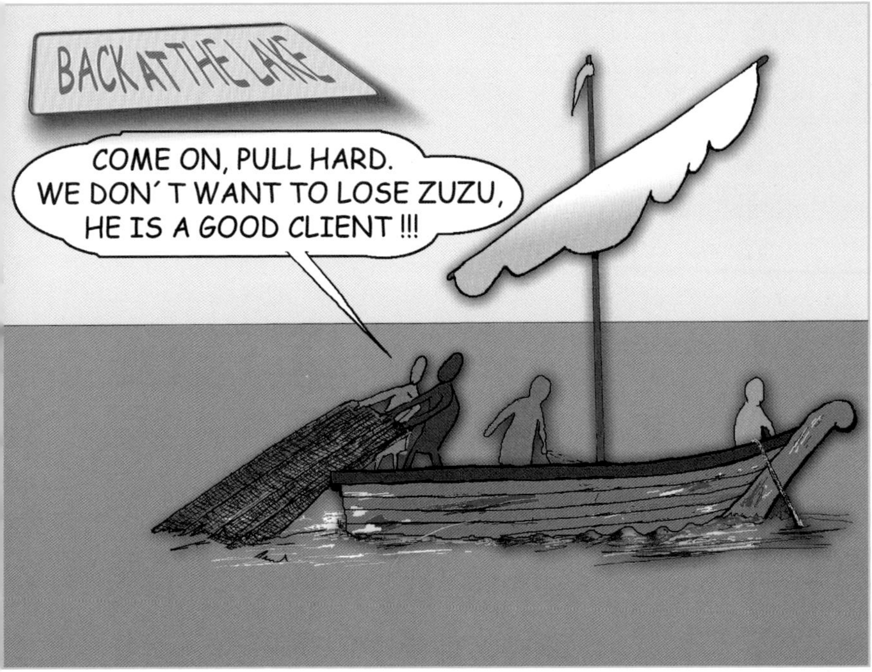
BACK AT THE LAKE
COME ON, PULL HARD. WE DON´T WANT TO LOSE ZUZU, HE IS A GOOD CLIENT !!!

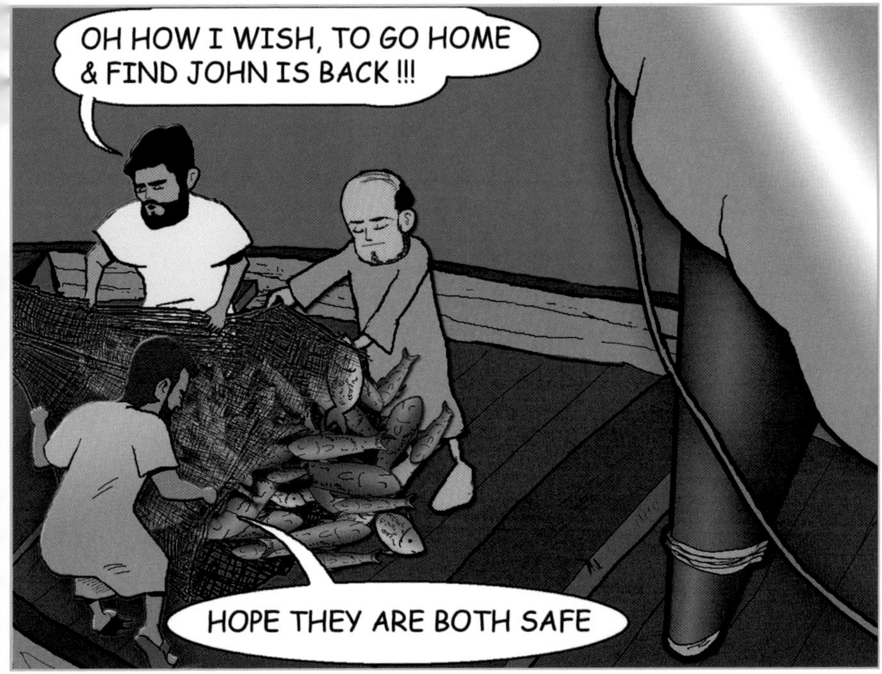
OH HOW I WISH, TO GO HOME & FIND JOHN IS BACK !!!
HOPE THEY ARE BOTH SAFE

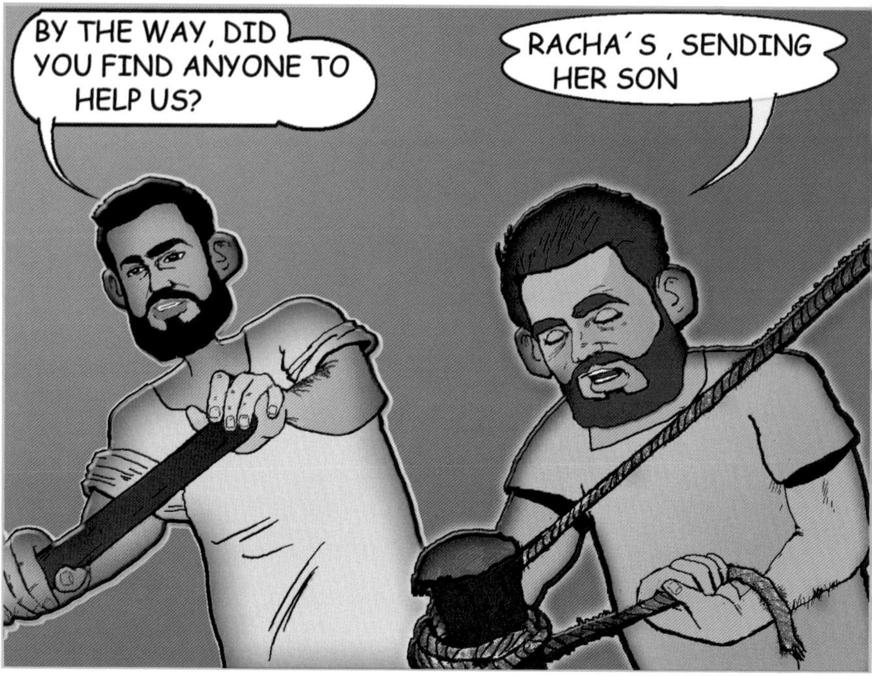
BY THE WAY, DID YOU FIND ANYONE TO HELP US?
RACHA´S , SENDING HER SON

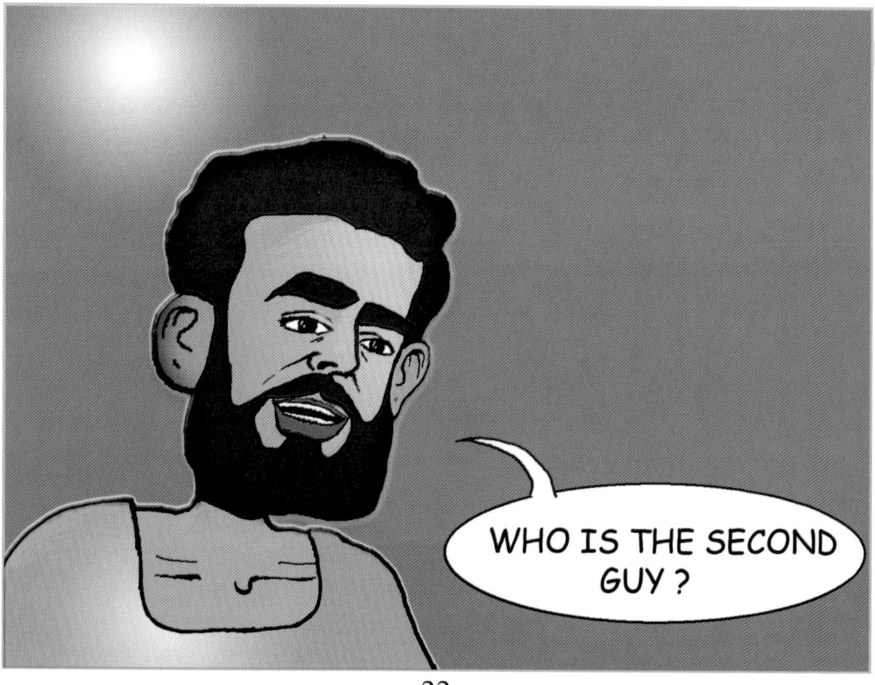
WHO IS THE SECOND GUY ?

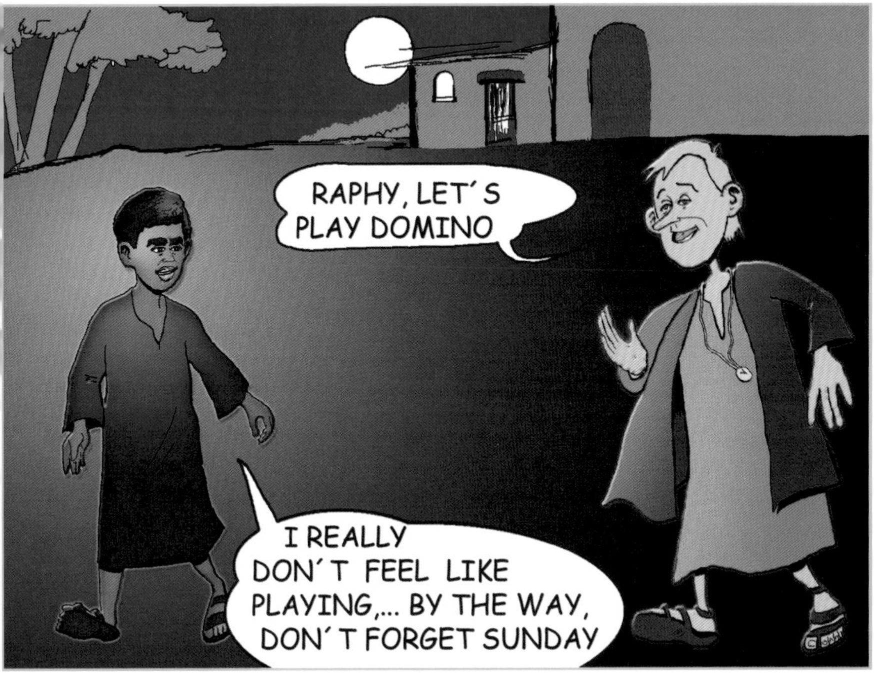
RAPHY, LET´S PLAY DOMINO
I REALLY DON´T FEEL LIKE PLAYING,... BY THE WAY, DON´T FORGET SUNDAY

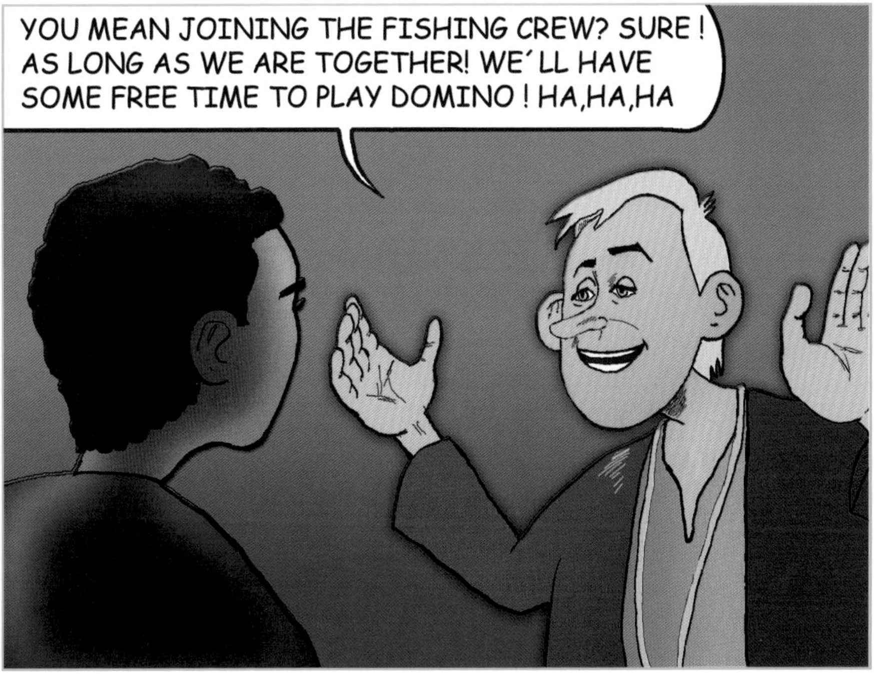
YOU MEAN JOINING THE FISHING CREW? SURE ! AS LONG AS WE ARE TOGETHER! WE´LL HAVE SOME FREE TIME TO PLAY DOMINO ! HA,HA,HA

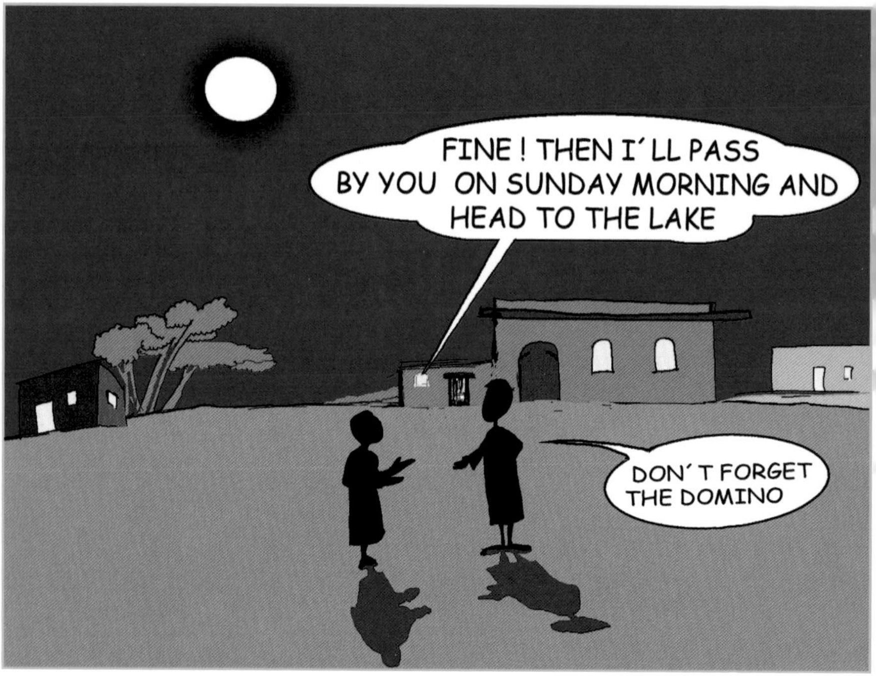
FINE ! THEN I´LL PASS BY YOU ON SUNDAY MORNING AND HEAD TO THE LAKE
DON´T FORGET THE DOMINO

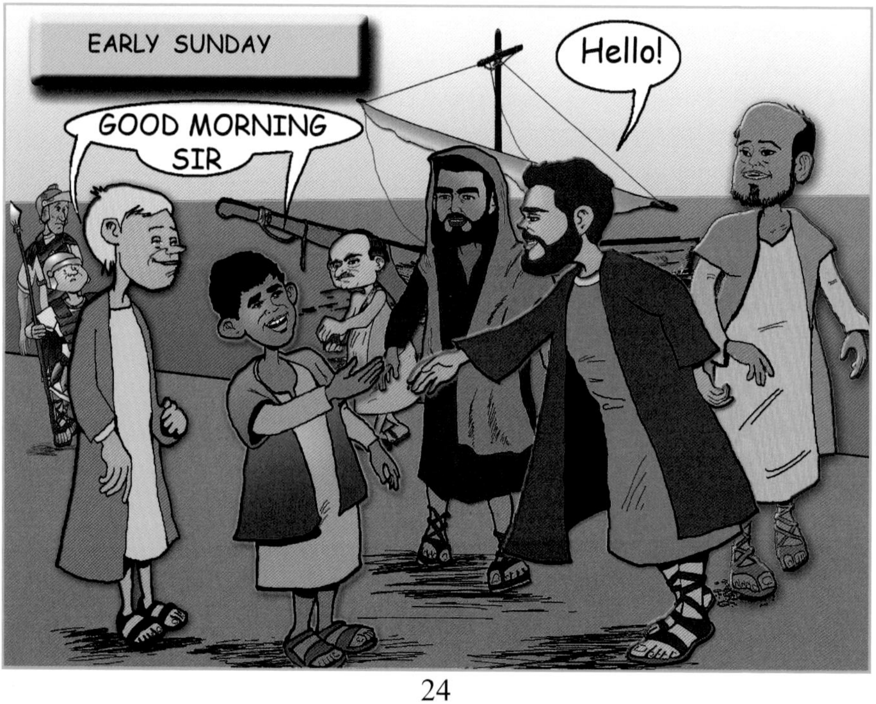
EARLY SUNDAY
GOOD MORNING SIR
Hello!

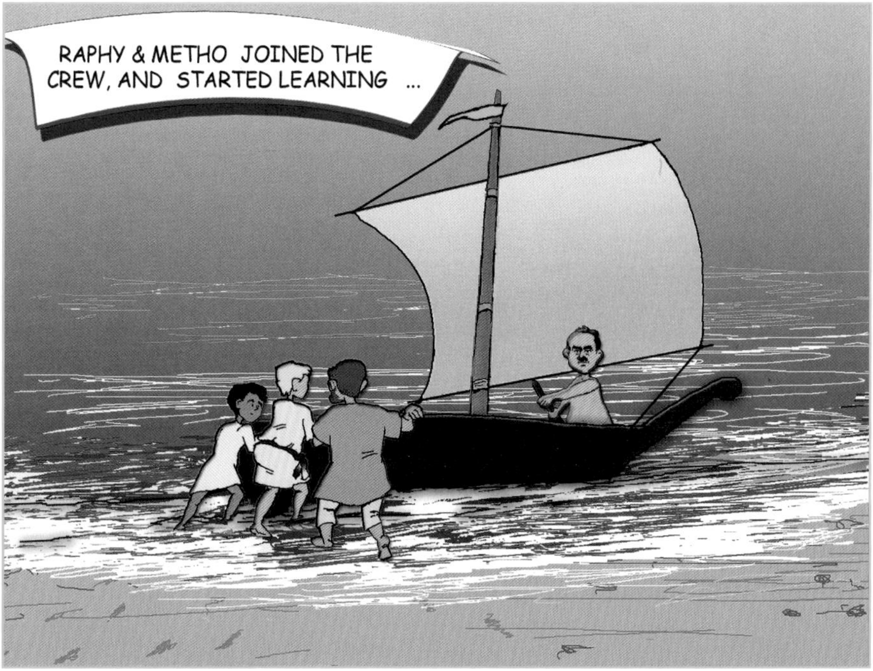
RAPHY & METHO JOINED THE CREW, AND STARTED LEARNING ...

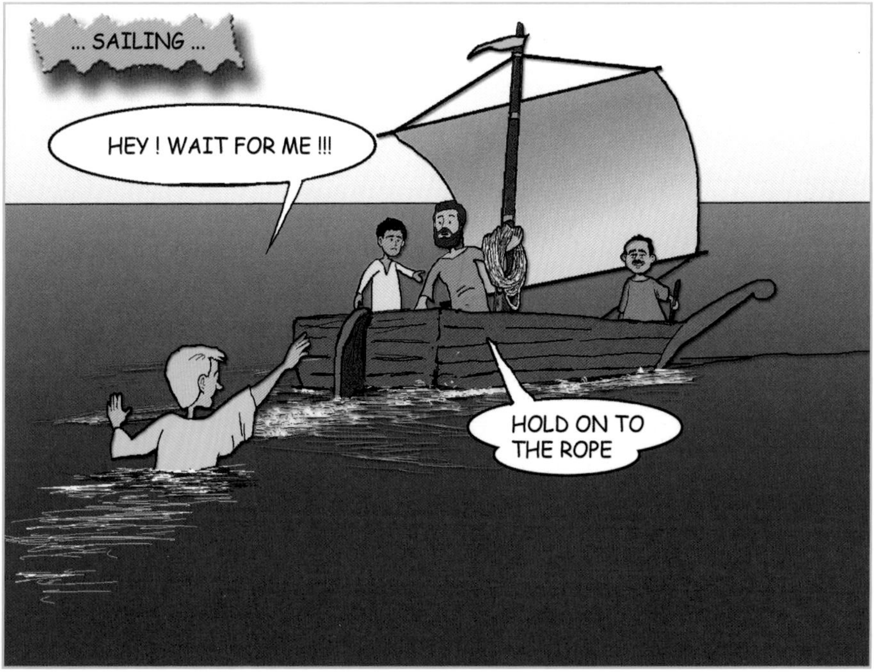
... SAILING ...
HEY ! WAIT FOR ME !!!
HOLD ON TO THE ROPE

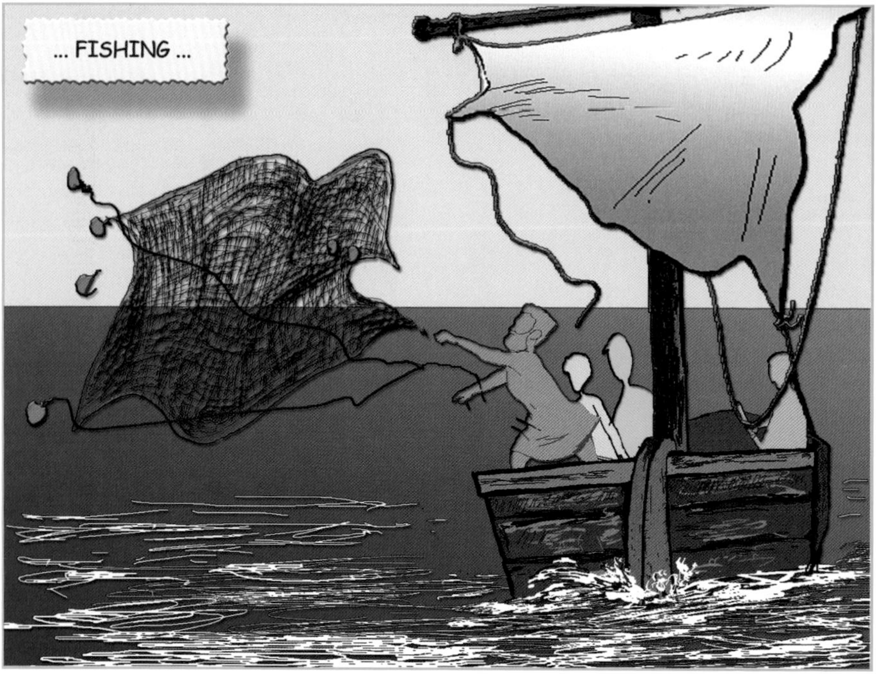
... FISHING ...

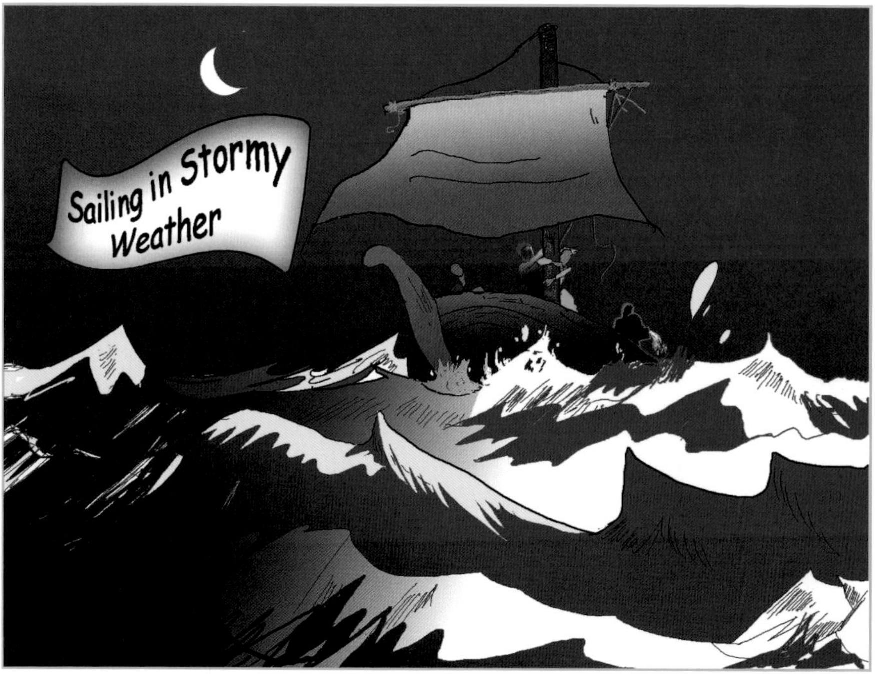
Sailing in Stormy Weather

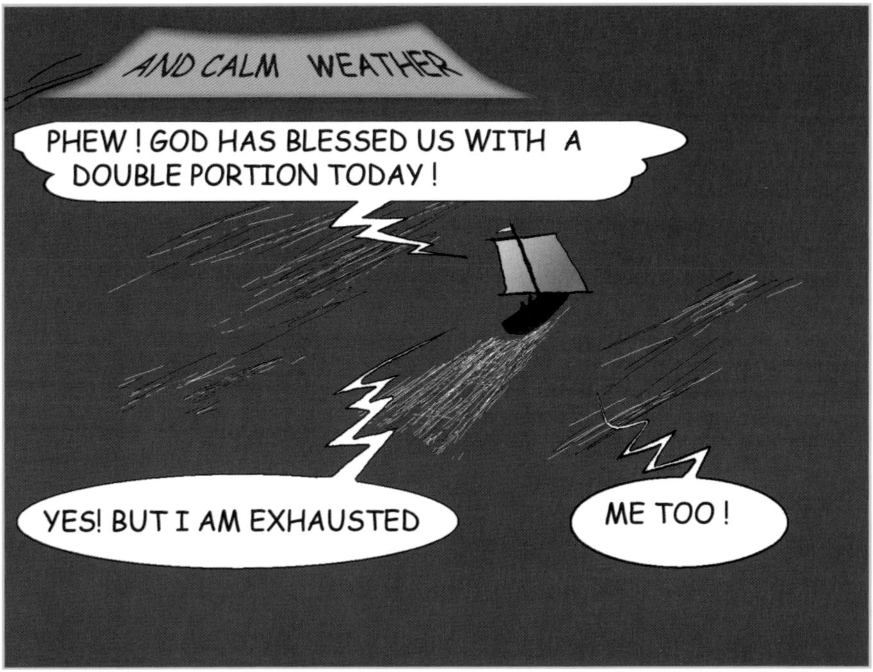
AND CALM WEATHER
PHEW ! GOD HAS BLESSED US WITH A DOUBLE PORTION TODAY !
YES! BUT I AM EXHAUSTED
ME TOO !

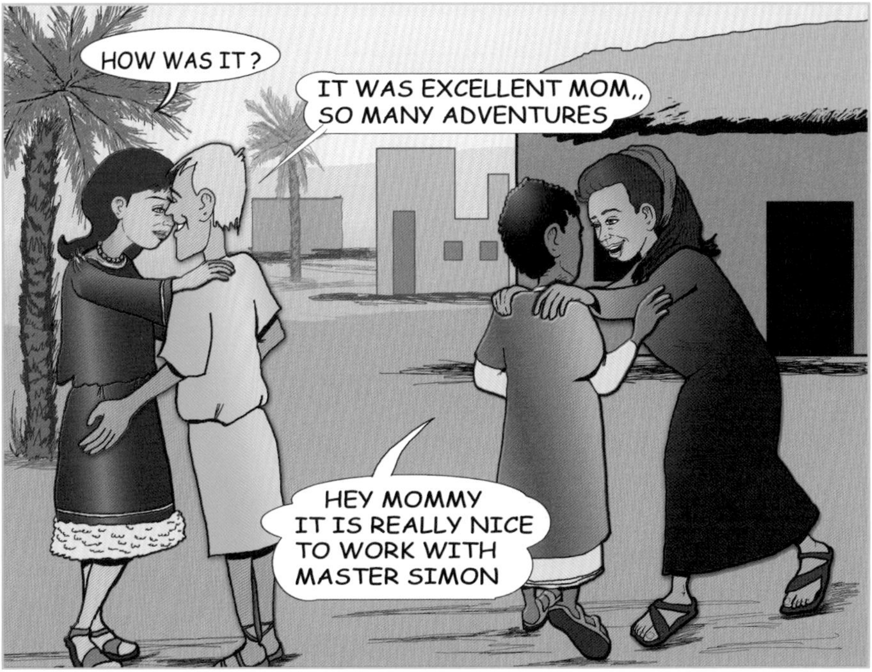
HOW WAS IT ?
IT WAS EXCELLENT MOM,, SO MANY ADVENTURES
HEY MOMMY IT IS REALLY NICE TO WORK WITH MASTER SIMON

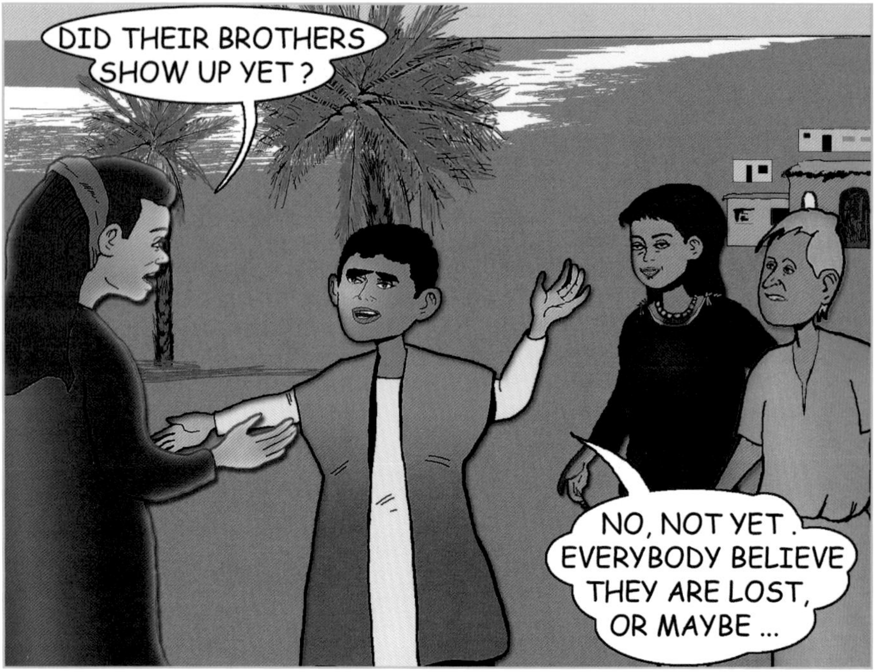
DID THEIR BROTHERS SHOW UP YET ?
NO, NOT YET . EVERYBODY BELIEVE THEY ARE LOST, OR MAYBE ...

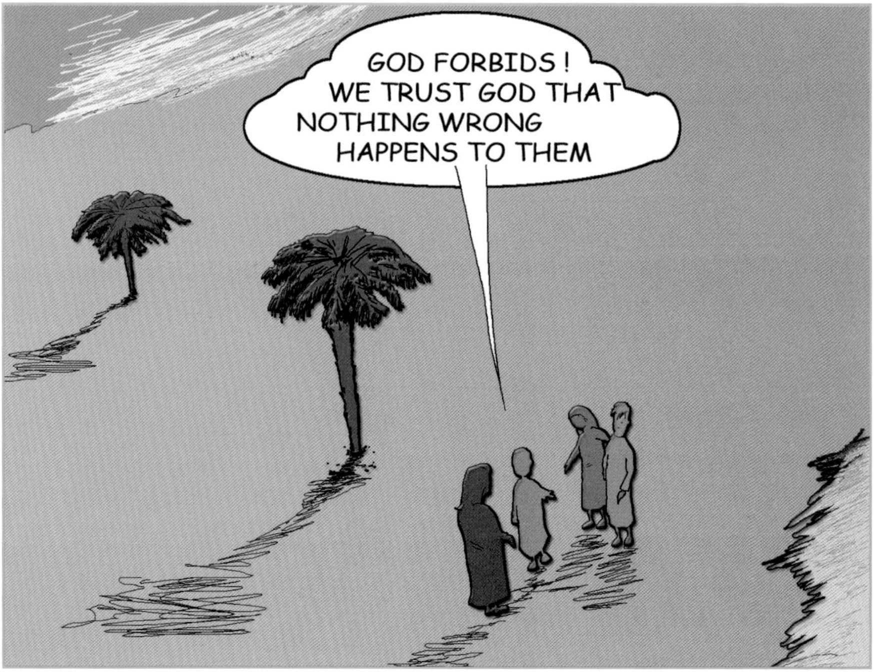
GOD FORBIDS ! WE TRUST GOD THAT NOTHING WRONG HAPPENS TO THEM

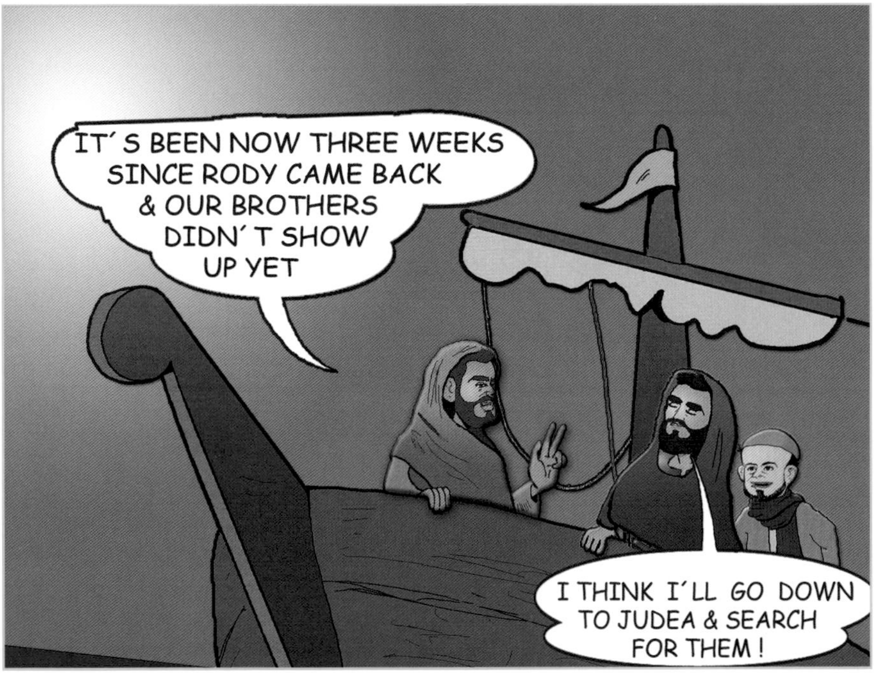
IT´S BEEN NOW THREE WEEKS SINCE RODY CAME BACK & OUR BROTHERS DIDN´T SHOW UP YET
I THINK I´LL GO DOWN TO JUDEA & SEARCH FOR THEM !

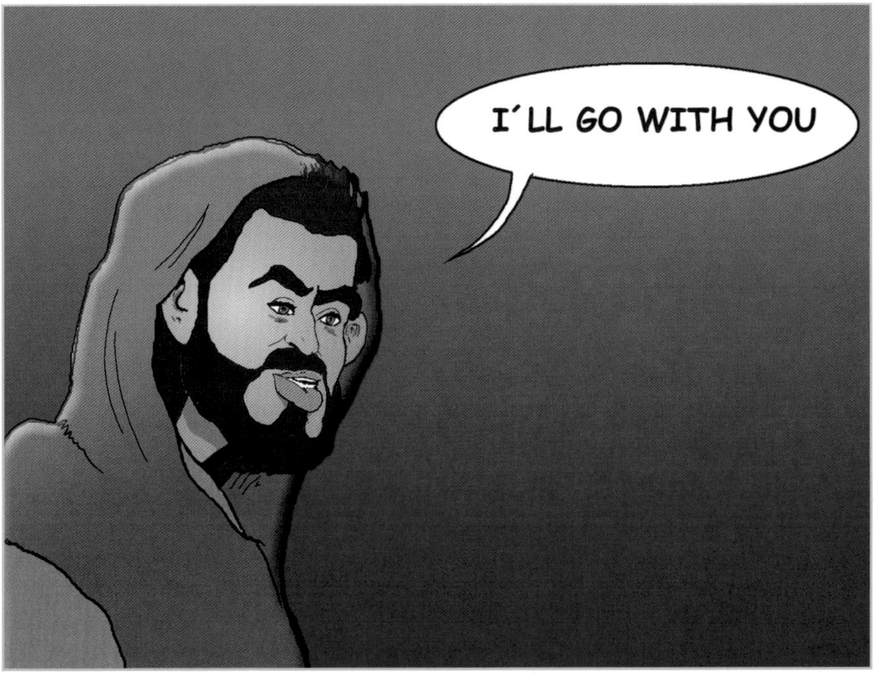
I´LL GO WITH YOU

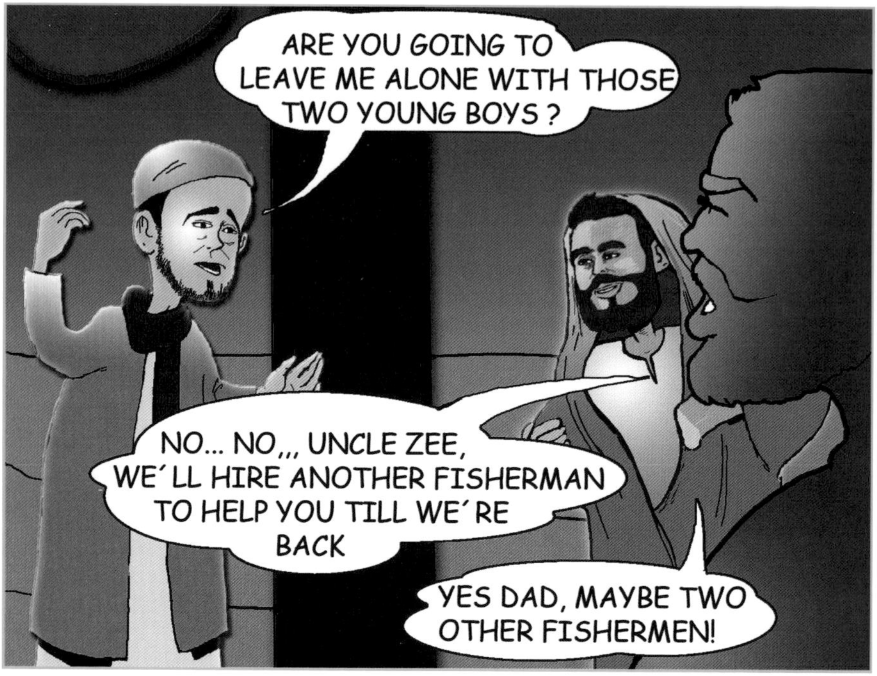
ARE YOU GOING TO LEAVE ME ALONE WITH THOSE TWO YOUNG BOYS ?
NO... NO,,, UNCLE ZEE, WE´LL HIRE ANOTHER FISHERMAN TO HELP YOU TILL WE´RE BACK
YES DAD, MAYBE TWO OTHER FISHERMEN!

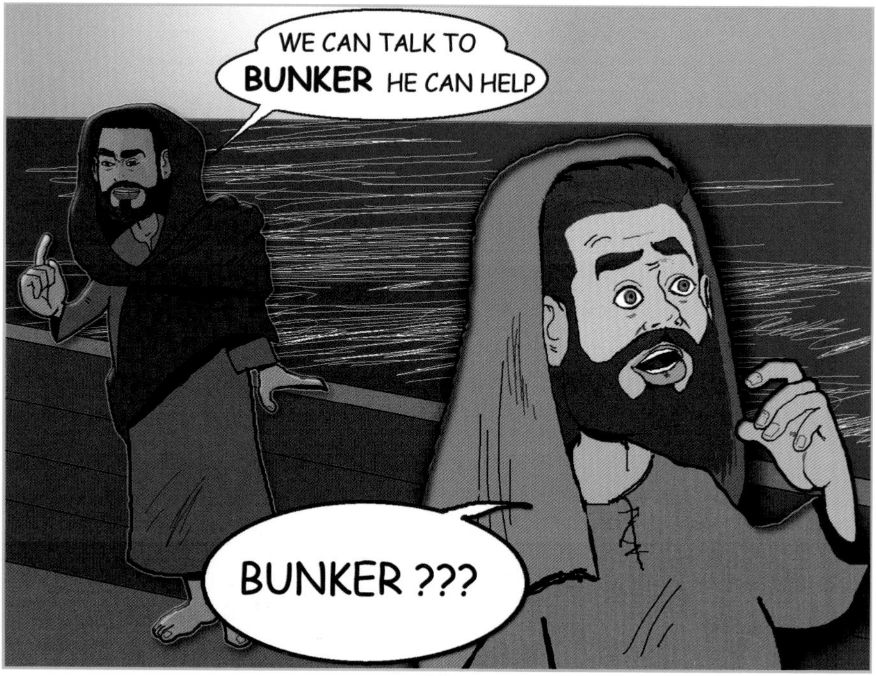
WE CAN TALK TO BUNKER HE CAN HELP
BUNKER ???

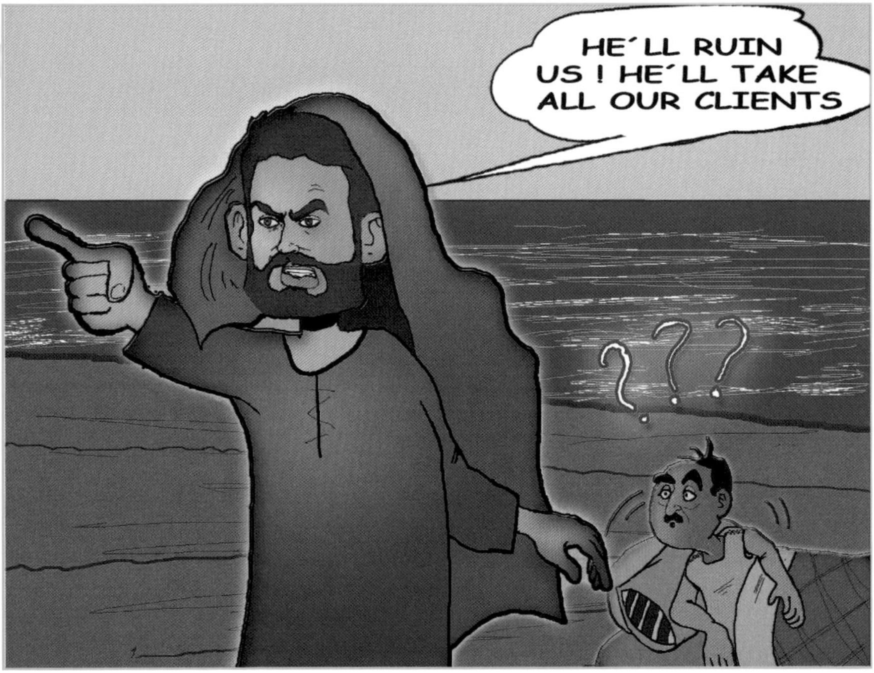
HE´LL RUIN US ! HE´LL TAKE ALL OUR CLIENTS

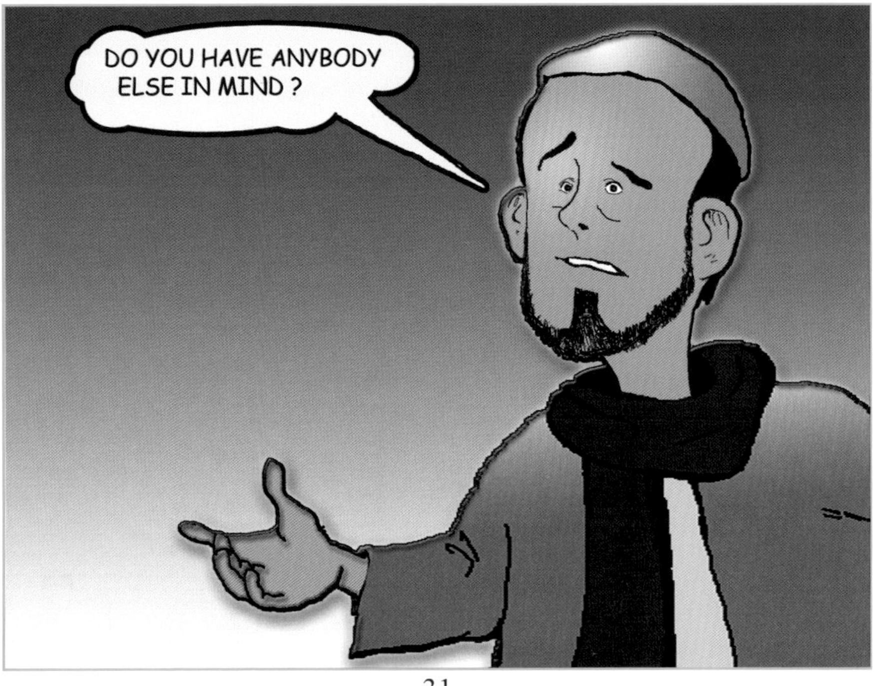
DO YOU HAVE ANYBODY ELSE IN MIND ?

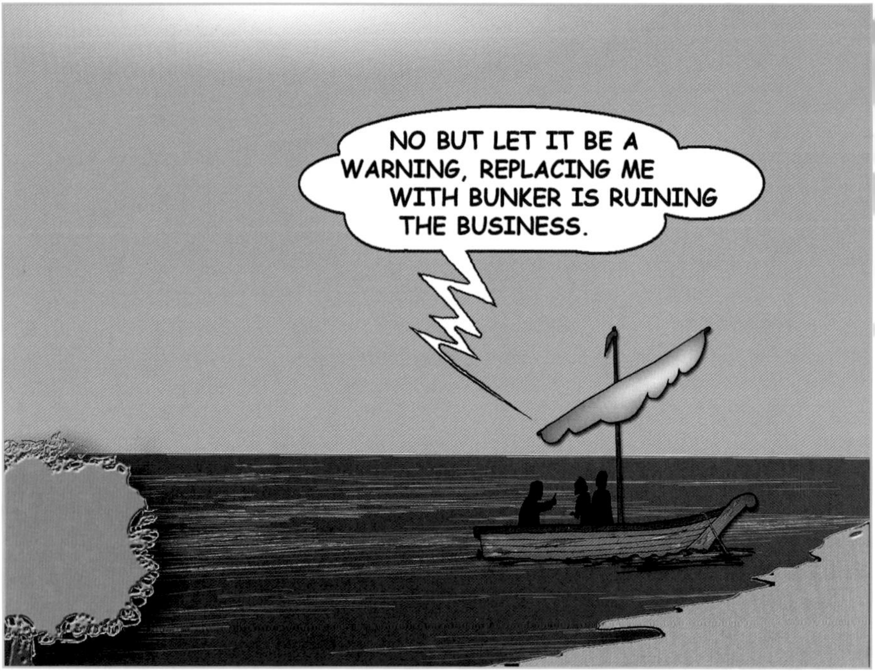
NO BUT LET IT BE A WARNING, REPLACING ME WITH BUNKER IS RUINING THE BUSINESS.

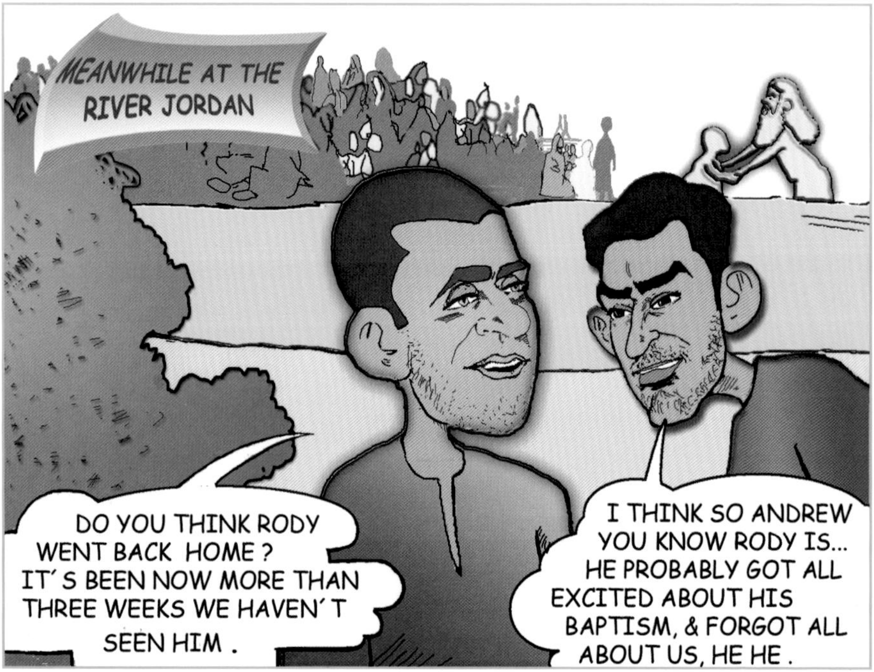
MEANWHILE AT THE RIVER JORDAN
DO YOU THINK RODY WENT BACK HOME ? IT´S BEEN NOW MORE THAN THREE WEEKS WE HAVEN´T SEEN HIM .
I THINK SO ANDREW YOU KNOW RODY IS... HE PROBABLY GOT ALL EXCITED ABOUT HIS BAPTISM, & FORGOT ALL ABOUT US, HE HE .

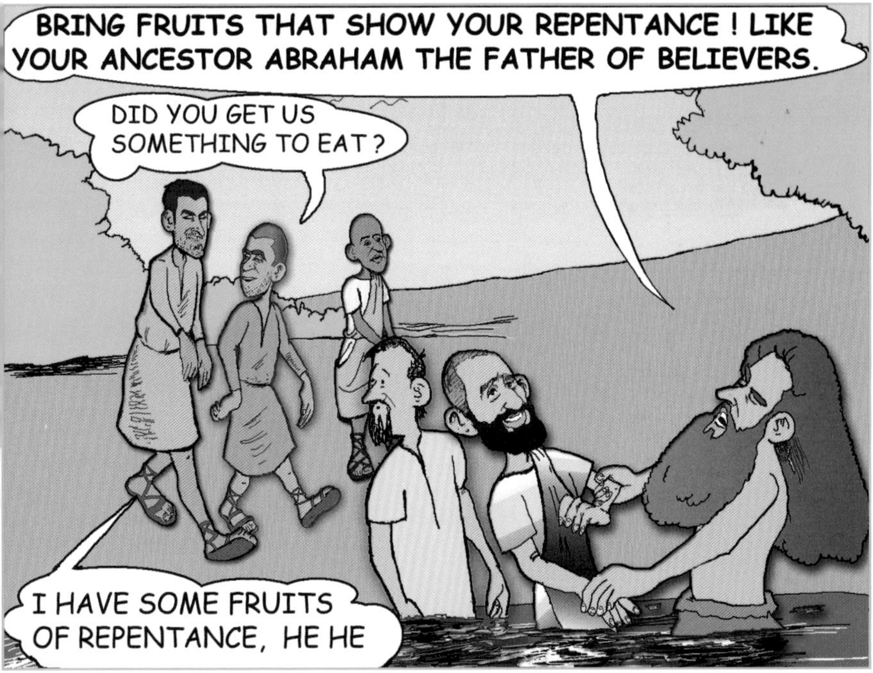
BRING FRUITS THAT SHOW YOUR REPENTANCE ! LIKE YOUR ANCESTOR ABRAHAM THE FATHER OF BELIEVERS.
DID YOU GET US SOMETHING TO EAT ?
I HAVE SOME FRUITS OF REPENTANCE, HE HE

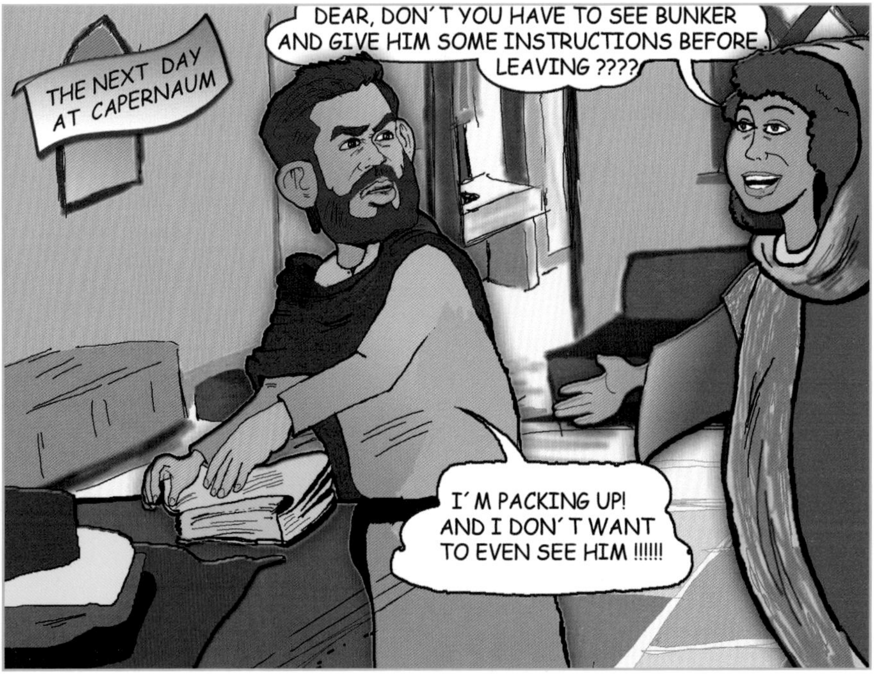
THE NEXT DAY AT CAPERNAUM
DEAR, DON´T YOU HAVE TO SEE BUNKER AND GIVE HIM SOME INSTRUCTIONS BEFORE LEAVING ????
I´M PACKING UP! AND I DON´T WANT TO EVEN SEE HIM !!!!!!

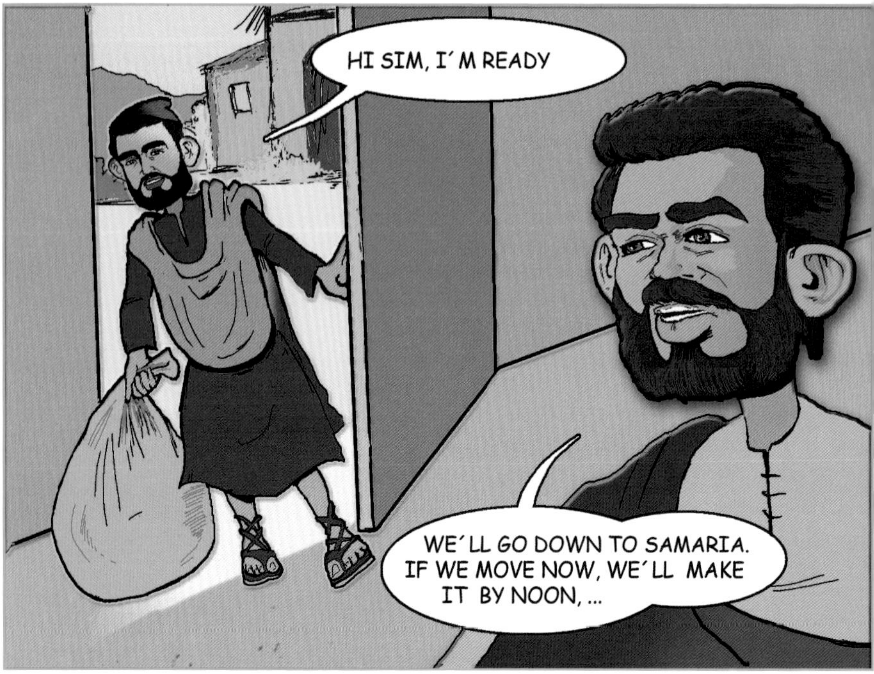
HI SIM, I´M READY
WE´LL GO DOWN TO SAMARIA. IF WE MOVE NOW, WE´LL MAKE IT BY NOON, ...

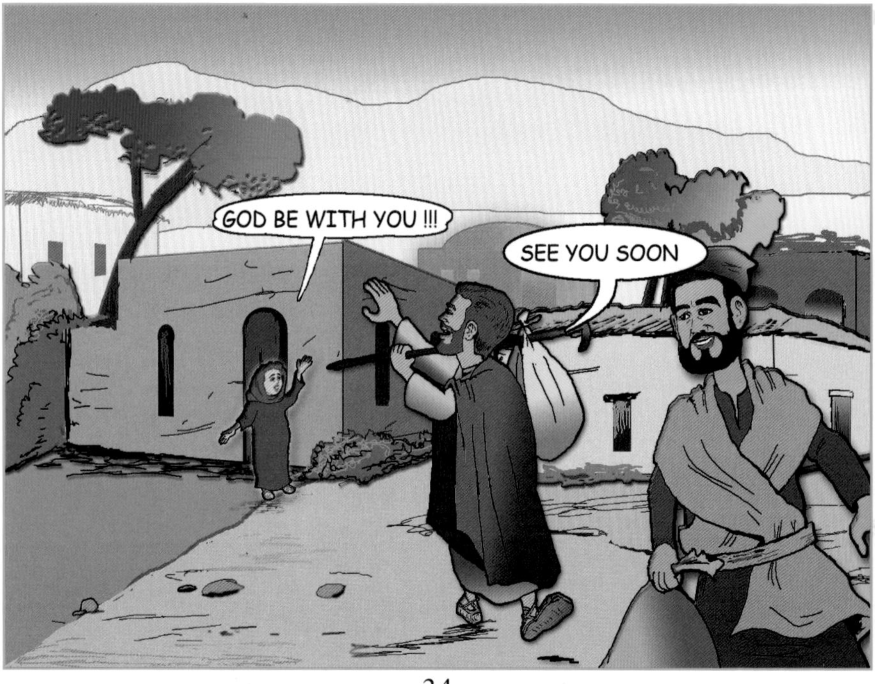
GOD BE WITH YOU !!!
SEE YOU SOON

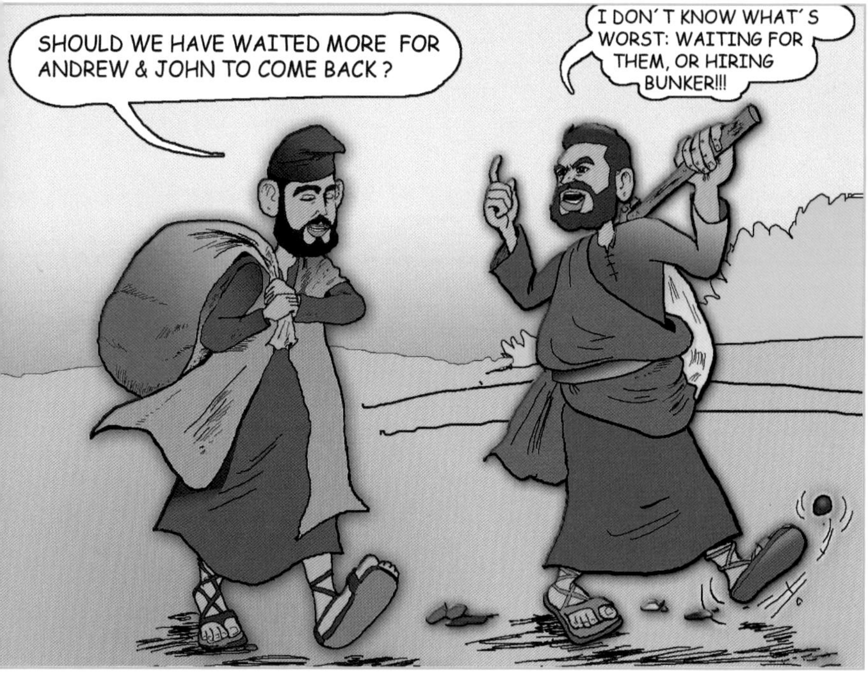
SHOULD WE HAVE WAITED MORE FOR ANDREW & JOHN TO COME BACK ?
I DON´T KNOW WHAT´S WORST: WAITING FOR THEM, OR HIRING BUNKER!!!

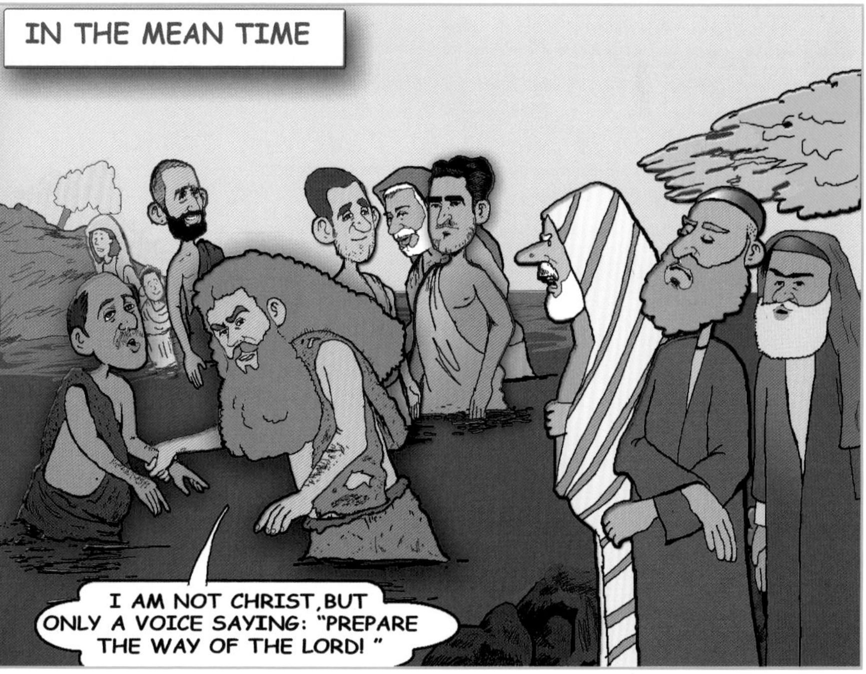
IN THE MEAN TIME
I AM NOT CHRIST, BUT ONLY A VOICE SAYING: "PREPARE THE WAY OF THE LORD! "

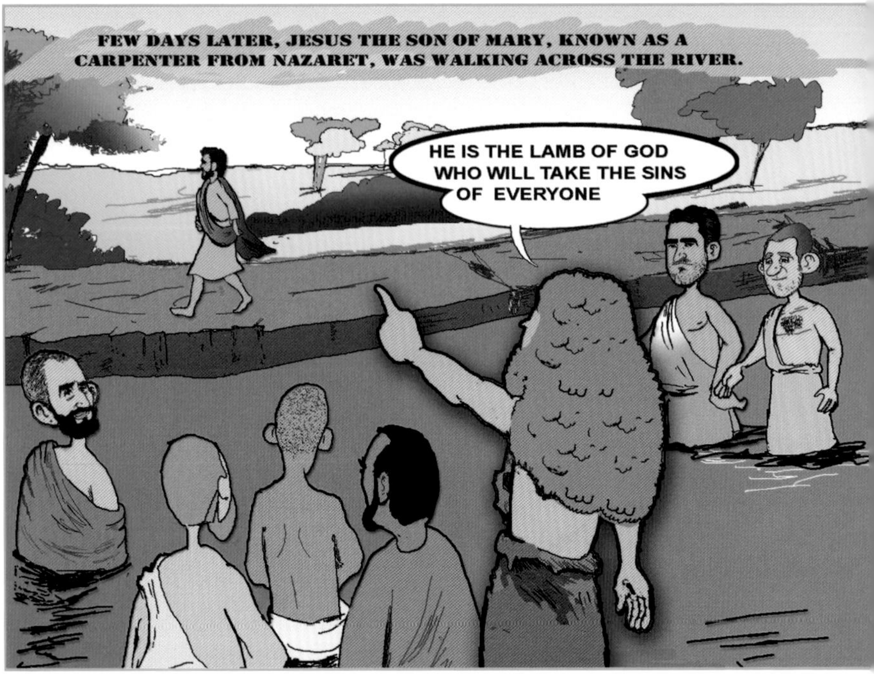
FEW DAYS LATER, JESUS THE SON OF MARY, KNOWN AS A CARPENTER FROM NAZARET, WAS WALKING ACROSS THE RIVER.
HE IS THE LAMB OF GOD WHO WILL TAKE THE SINS OF EVERYONE

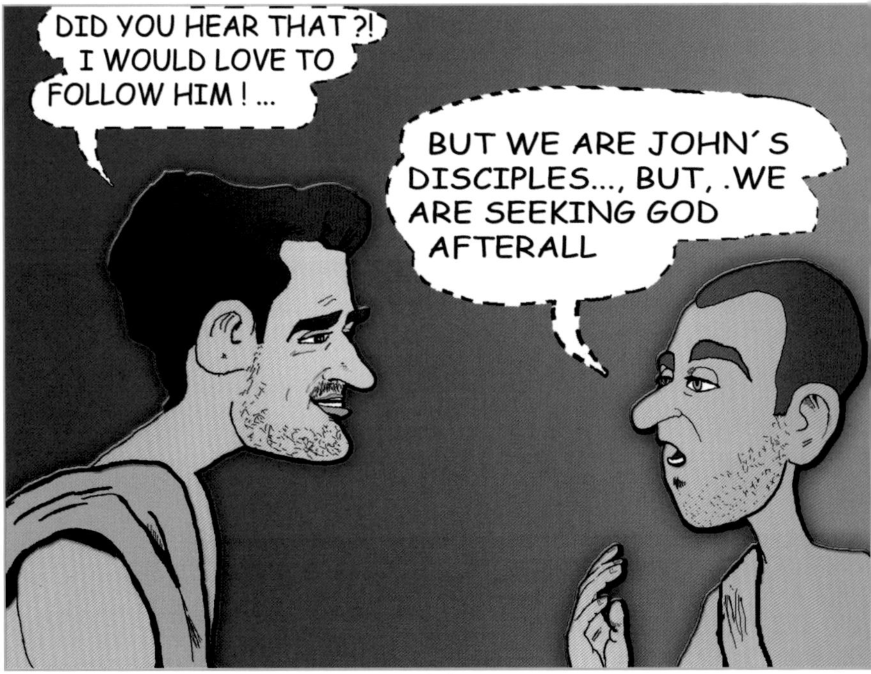
DID YOU HEAR THAT ?! I WOULD LOVE TO FOLLOW HIM ! ...
BUT WE ARE JOHN´S DISCIPLES..., BUT, .WE ARE SEEKING GOD AFTERALL

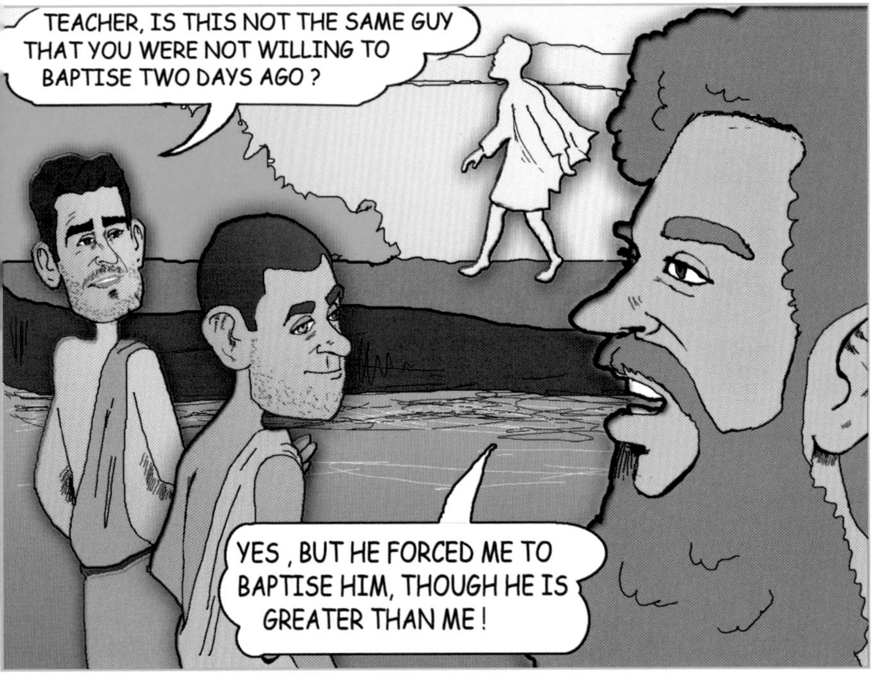
TEACHER, IS THIS NOT THE SAME GUY THAT YOU WERE NOT WILLING TO BAPTISE TWO DAYS AGO ?
YES , BUT HE FORCED ME TO BAPTISE HIM, THOUGH HE IS GREATER THAN ME !

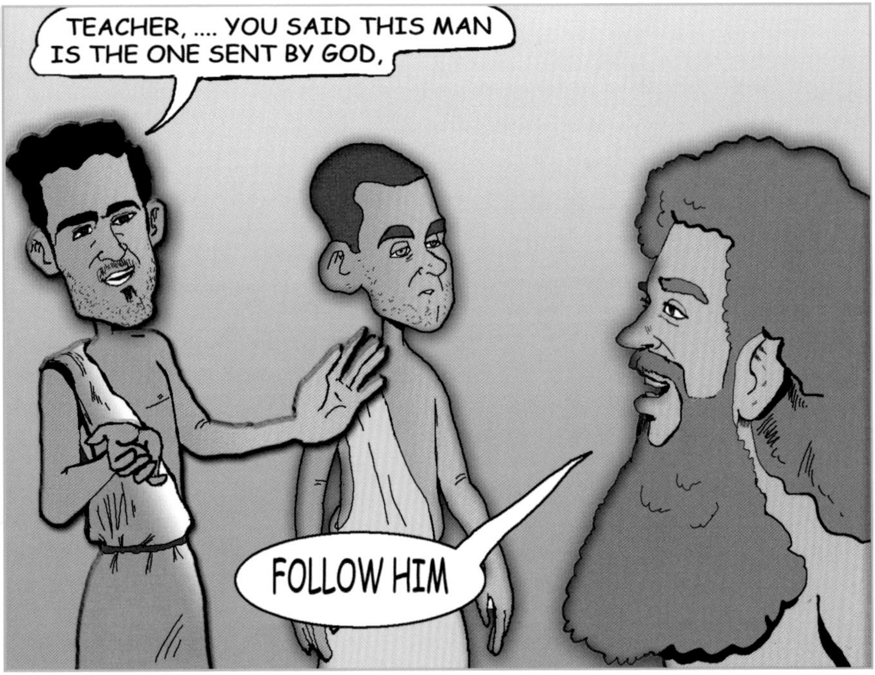
TEACHER, ... YOU SAID THIS MAN IS THE ONE SENT BY GOD,
FOLLOW HIM

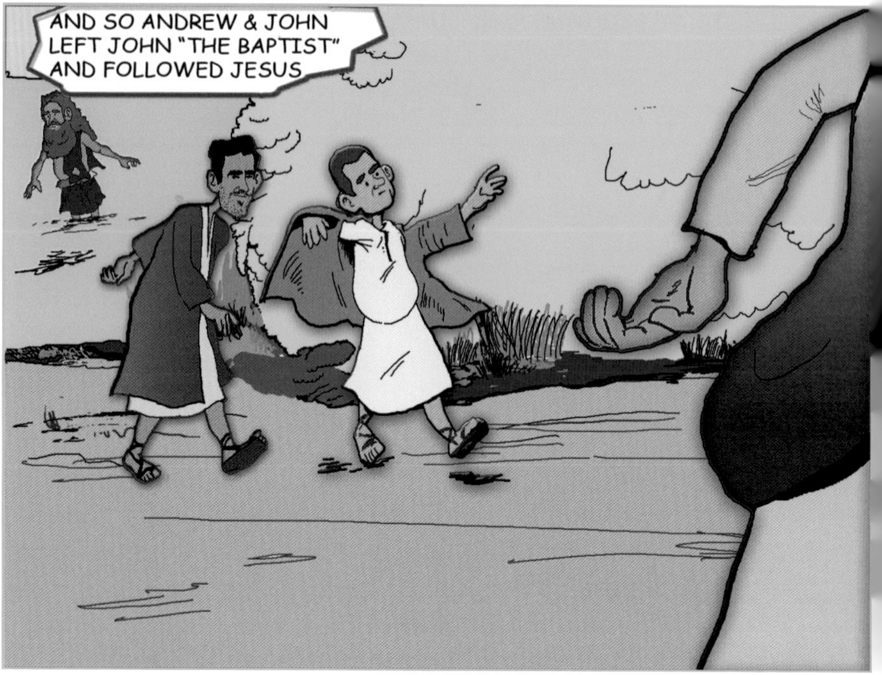
AND SO ANDREW & JOHN LEFT JOHN "THE BAPTIST" AND FOLLOWED JESUS

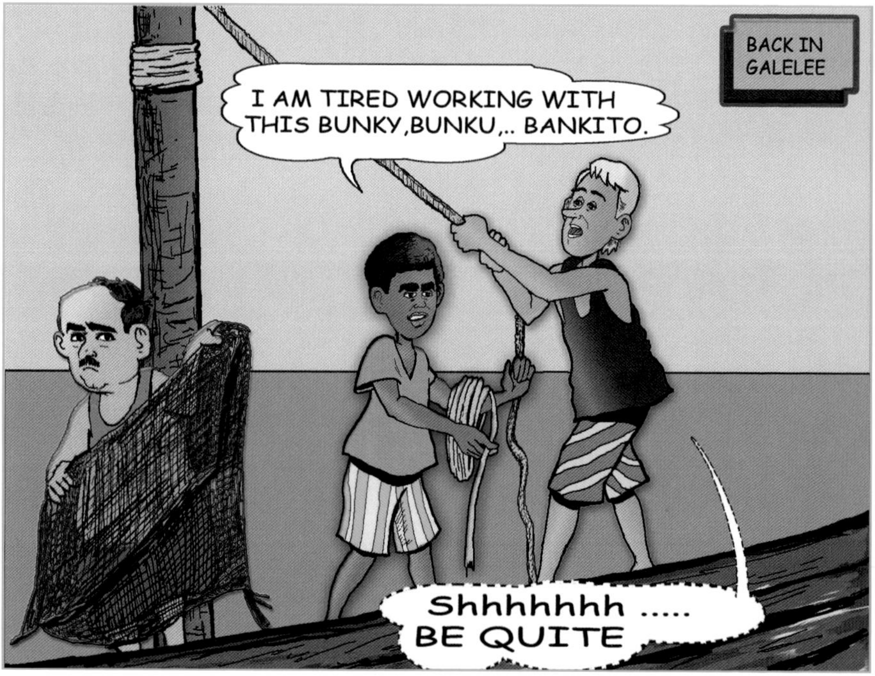
BACK IN GALELEE
I AM TIRED WORKING WITH THIS BUNKY,BUNKU,.. BANKITO.
Shhhhhhh ..... BE QUITE

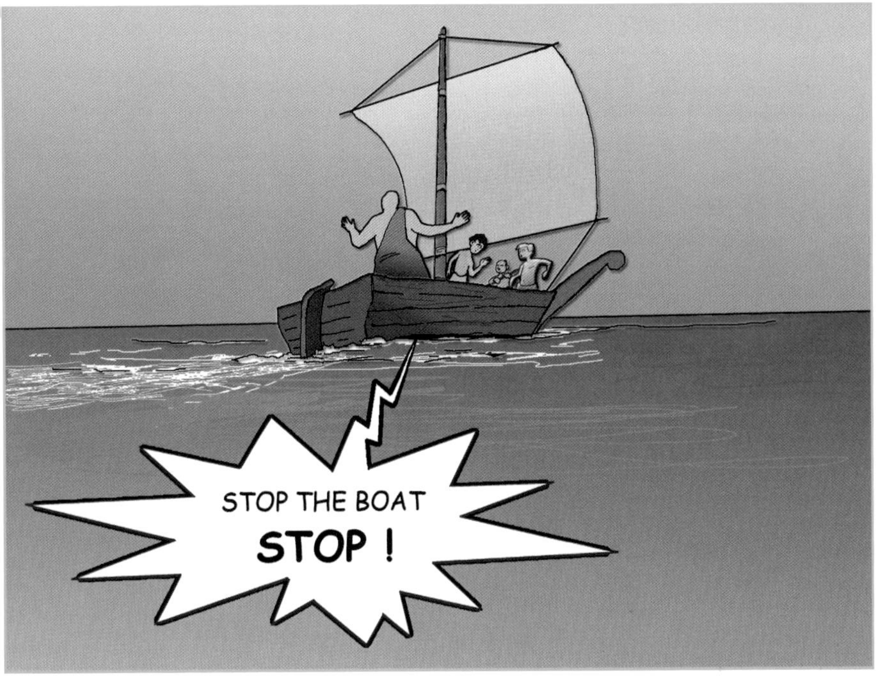
STOP THE BOAT
STOP !

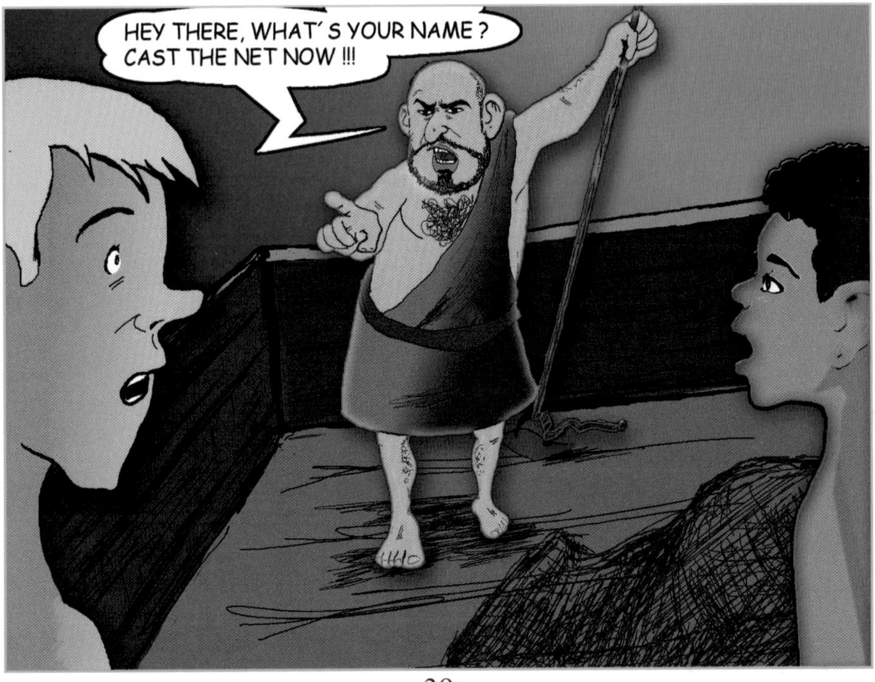
HEY THERE, WHAT´S YOUR NAME ?
CAST THE NET NOW !!!

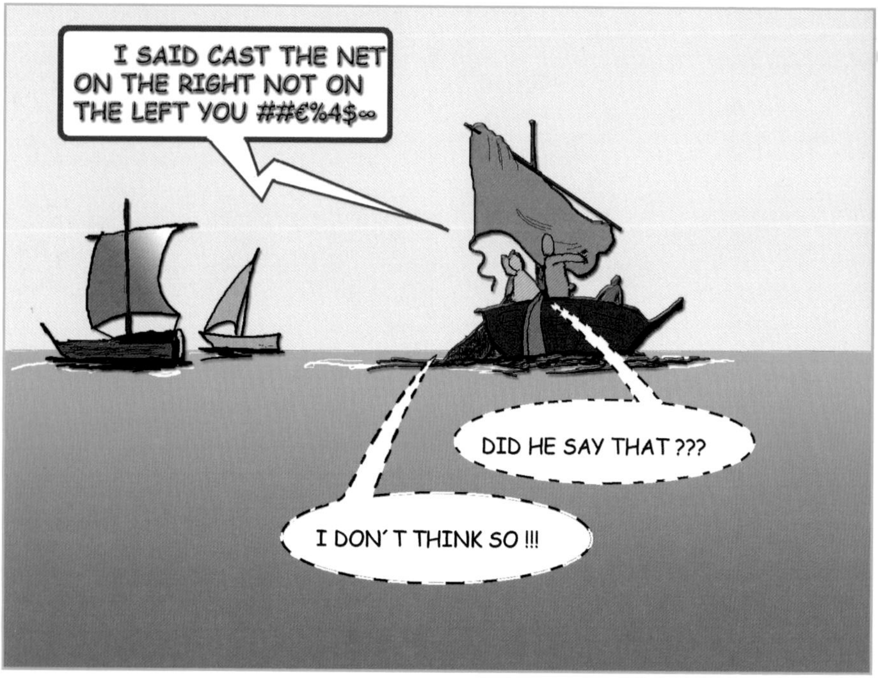
I SAID CAST THE NET ON THE RIGHT NOT ON THE LEFT YOU ##€%4$∞
DID HE SAY THAT ???
I DON´T THINK SO !!!

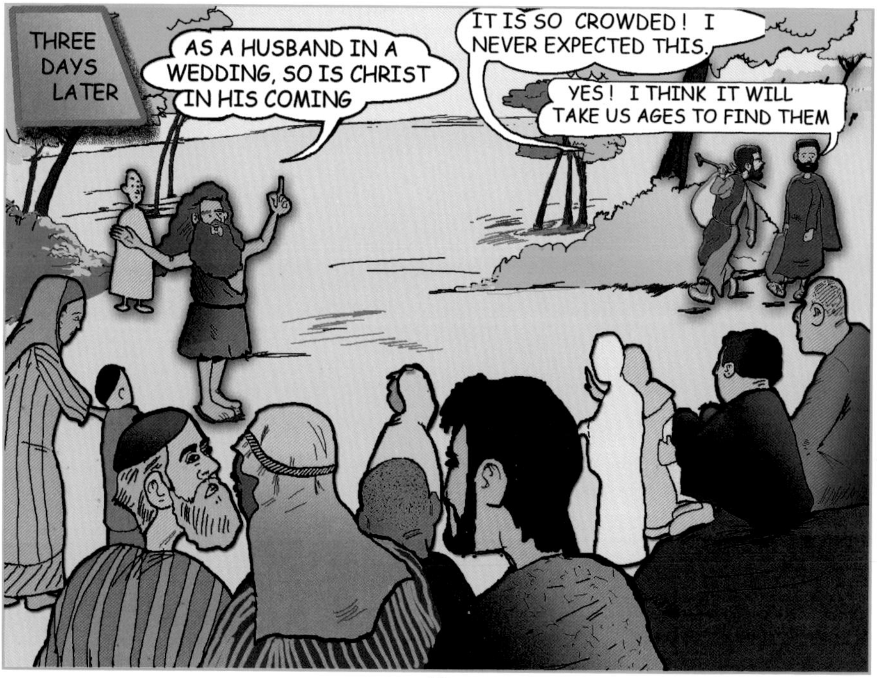
THREE DAYS LATER
AS A HUSBAND IN A WEDDING, SO IS CHRIST IN HIS COMING
IT IS SO CROWDED ! I NEVER EXPECTED THIS.
YES ! I THINK IT WILL TAKE US AGES TO FIND THEM

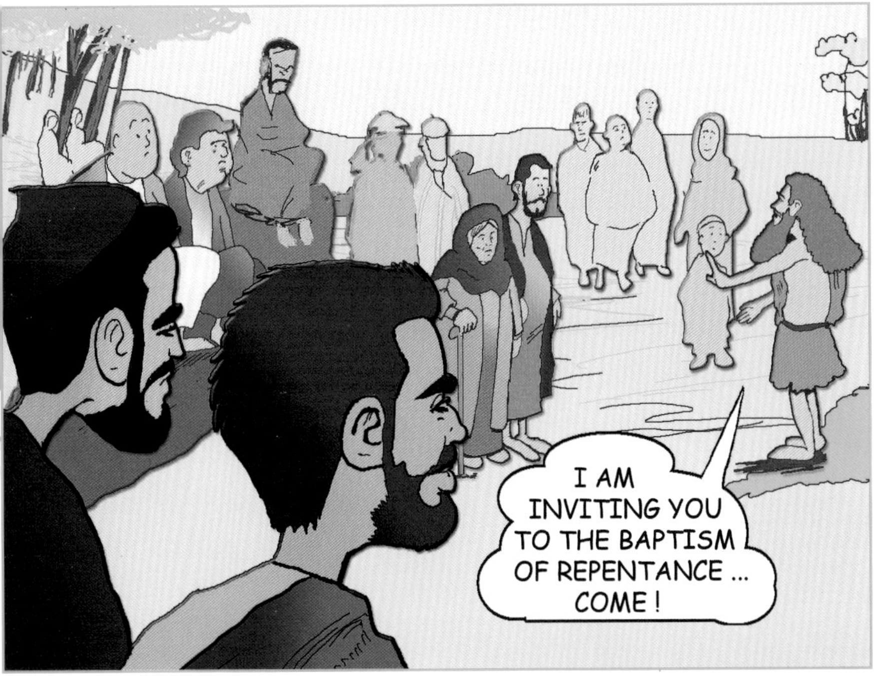
I AM INVITING YOU TO THE BAPTISM OF REPENTANCE ... COME !

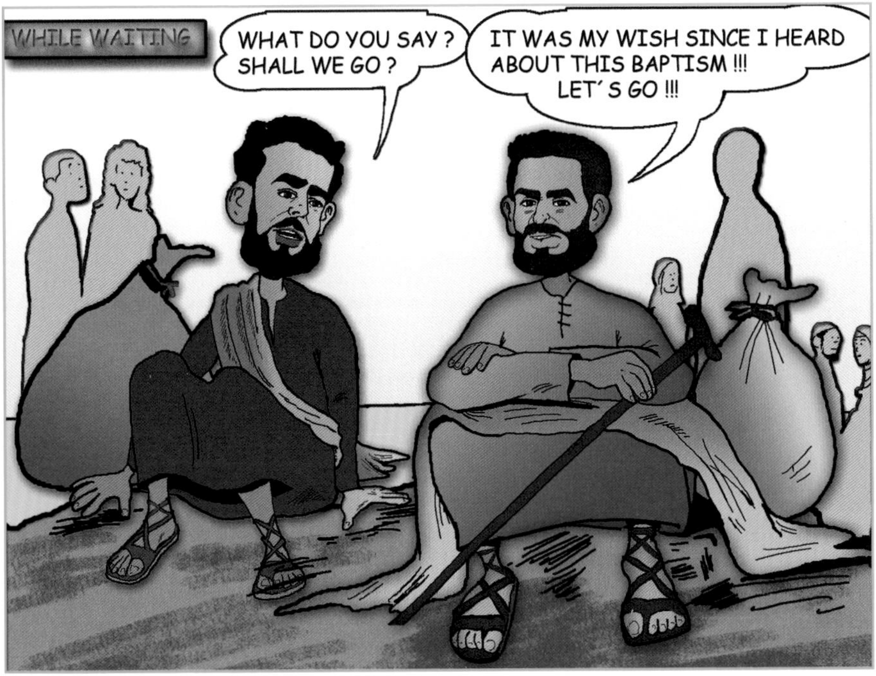
WHILE WAITING
WHAT DO YOU SAY ? SHALL WE GO ?
IT WAS MY WISH SINCE I HEARD ABOUT THIS BAPTISM !!! LET´S GO !!!

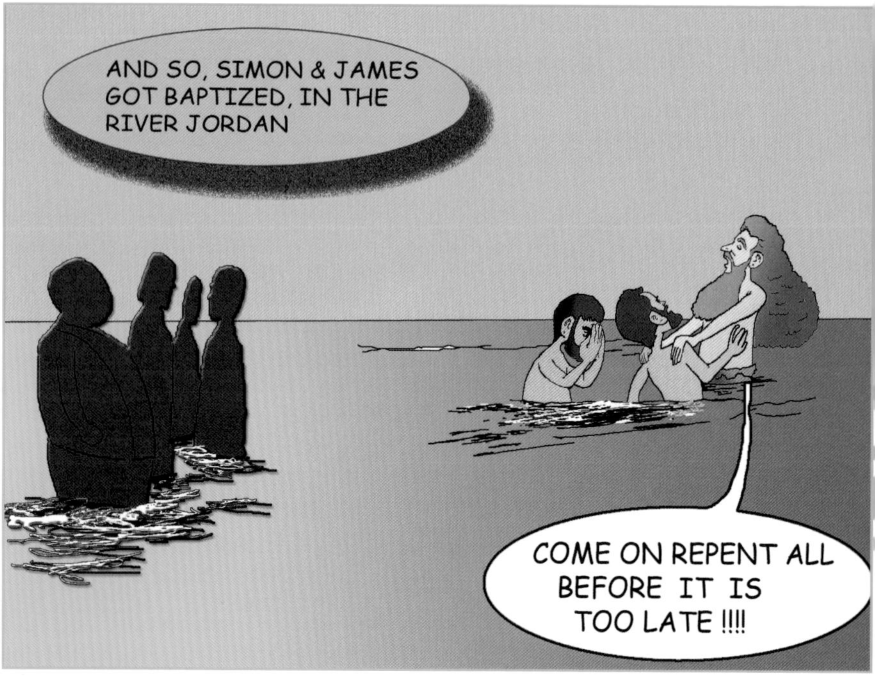
AND SO, SIMON & JAMES GOT BAPTIZED, IN THE RIVER JORDAN
COME ON REPENT ALL BEFORE IT IS TOO LATE !!!!

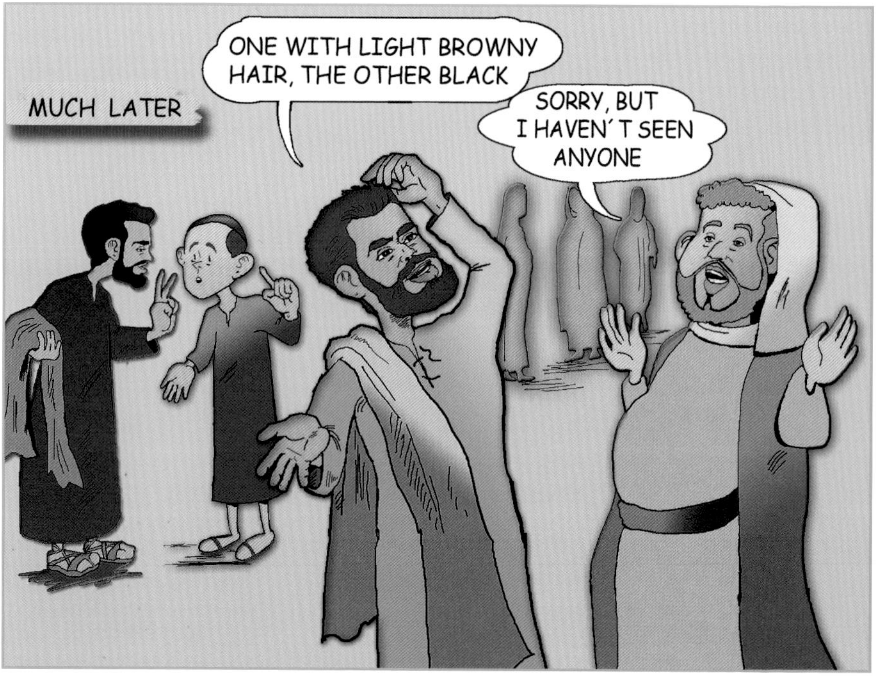
MUCH LATER
ONE WITH LIGHT BROWNY HAIR, THE OTHER BLACK
SORRY, BUT I HAVEN´T SEEN ANYONE

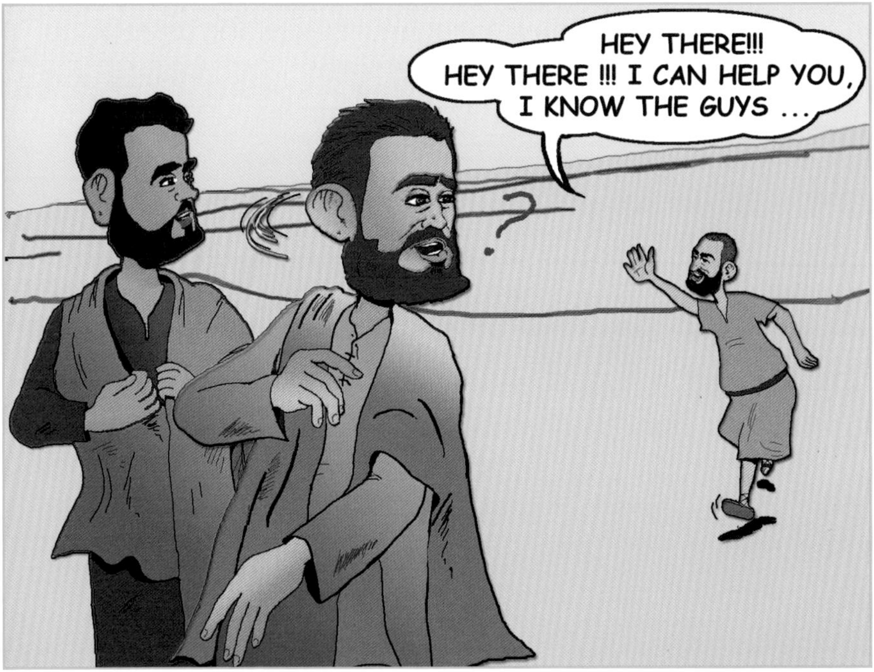
HEY THERE!!!
HEY THERE !!! I CAN HELP YOU,
I KNOW THE GUYS ...

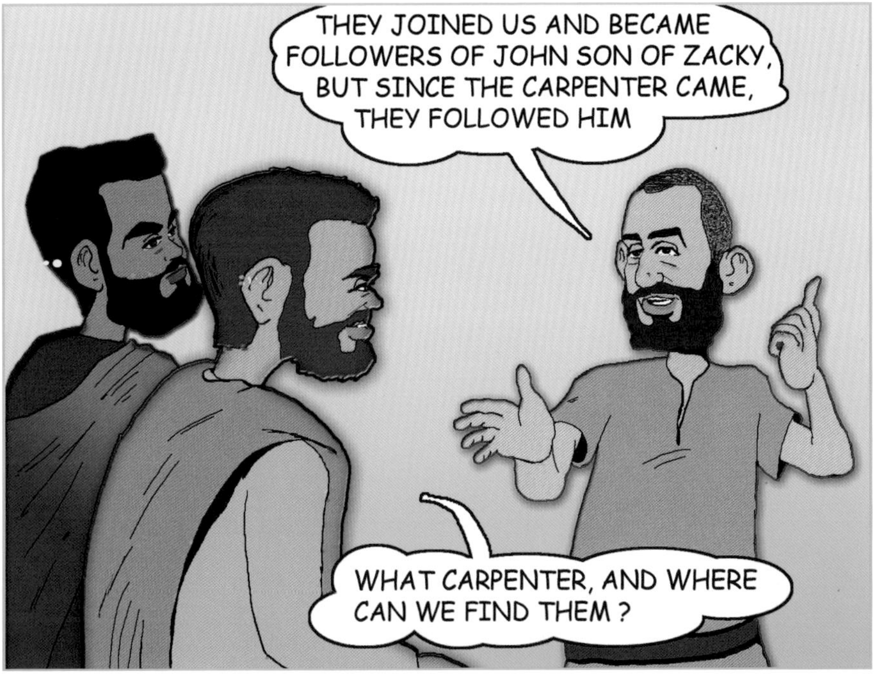
THEY JOINED US AND BECAME
FOLLOWERS OF JOHN SON OF ZACKY,
BUT SINCE THE CARPENTER CAME,
THEY FOLLOWED HIM
WHAT CARPENTER, AND WHERE
CAN WE FIND THEM ?

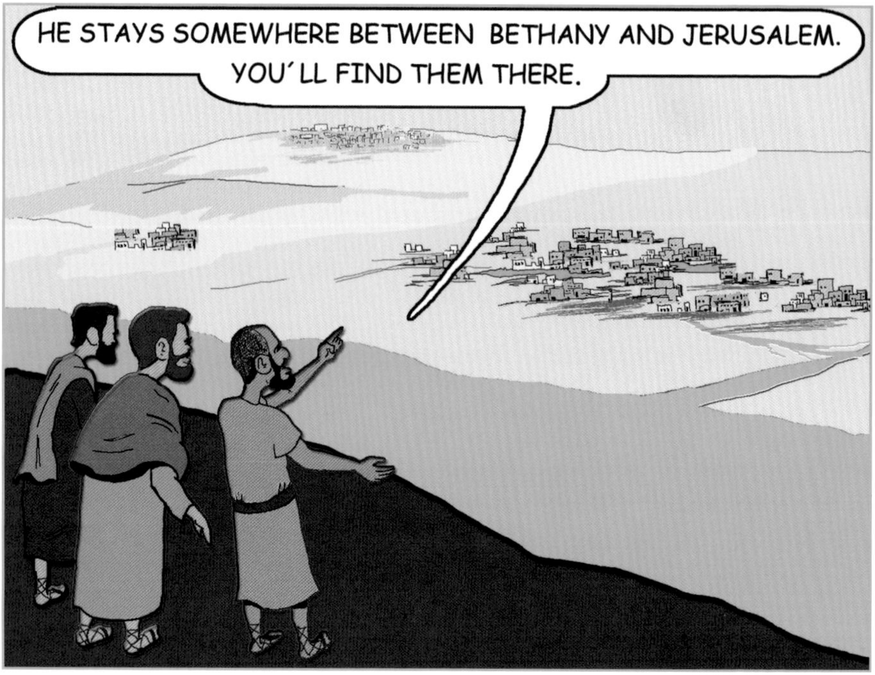
HE STAYS SOMEWHERE BETWEEN BETHANY AND JERUSALEM.
YOU´LL FIND THEM THERE.

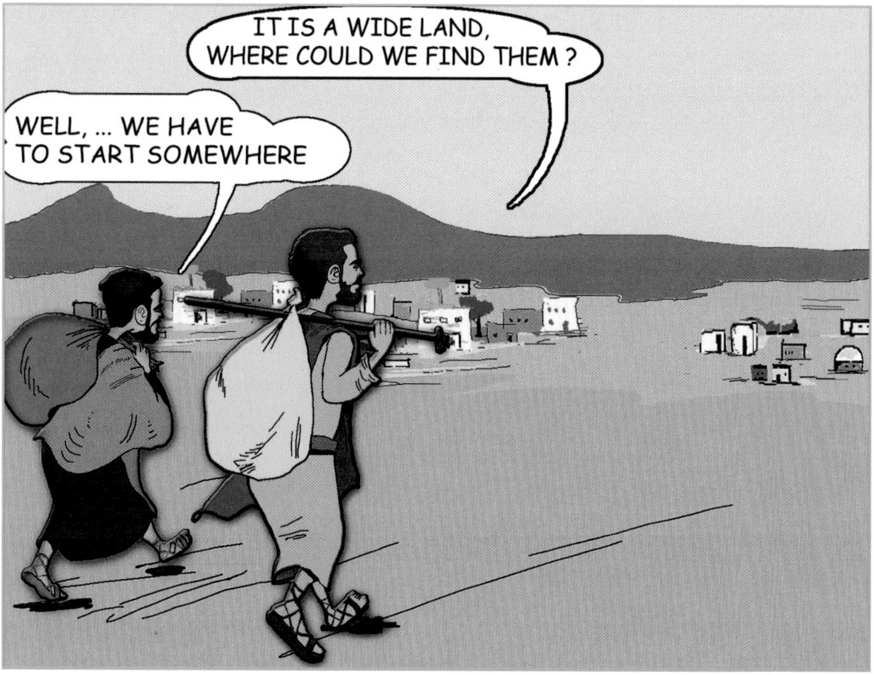
IT IS A WIDE LAND,
WHERE COULD WE FIND THEM ?
WELL, ... WE HAVE
TO START SOMEWHERE

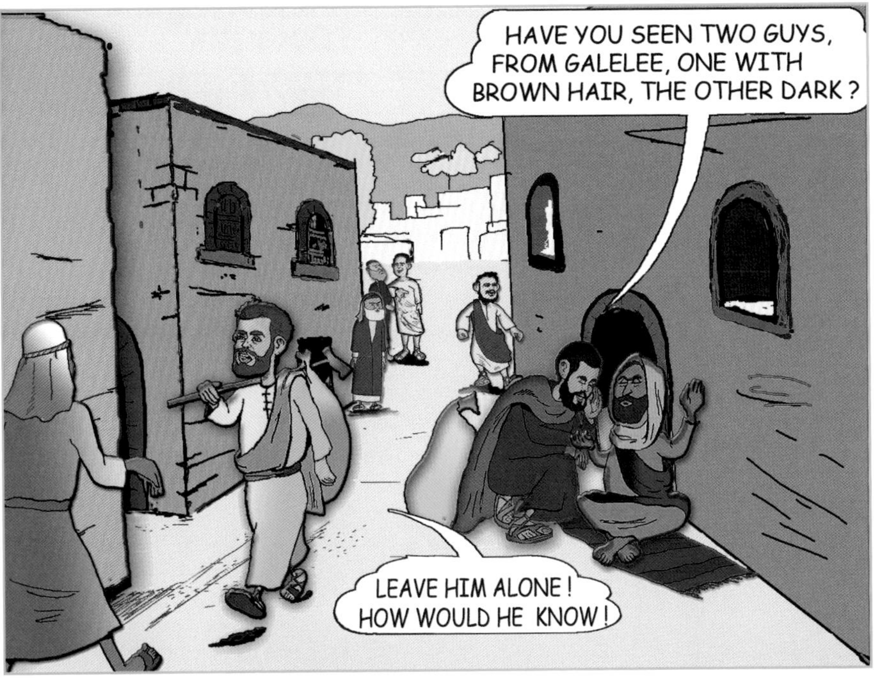
HAVE YOU SEEN TWO GUYS, FROM GALELEE, ONE WITH BROWN HAIR, THE OTHER DARK ?
LEAVE HIM ALONE ! HOW WOULD HE KNOW !

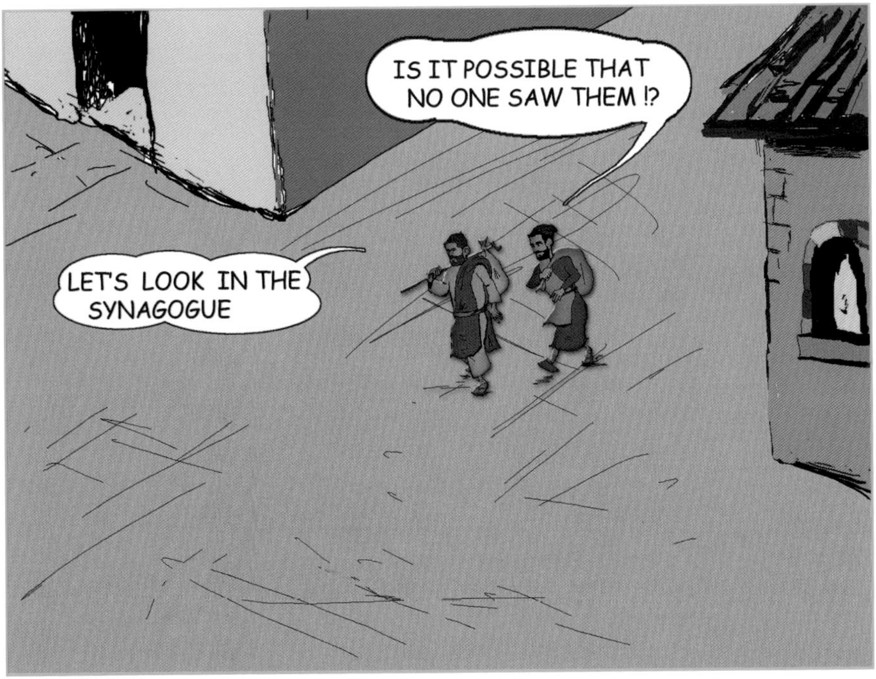
IS IT POSSIBLE THAT NO ONE SAW THEM !?
LET'S LOOK IN THE SYNAGOGUE

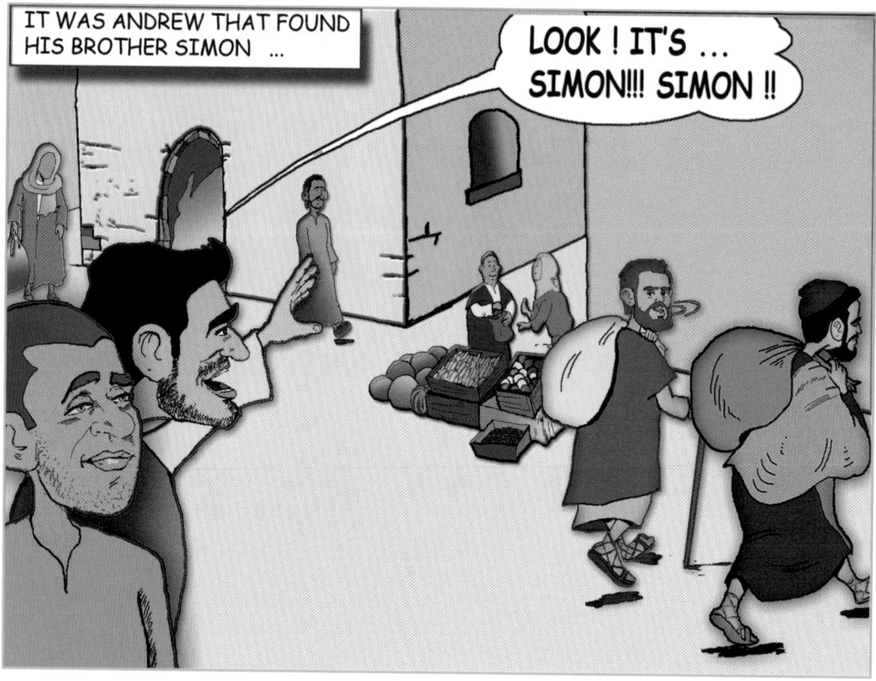
IT WAS ANDREW THAT FOUND HIS BROTHER SIMON ...
LOOK ! IT'S ... SIMON!!! SIMON !!

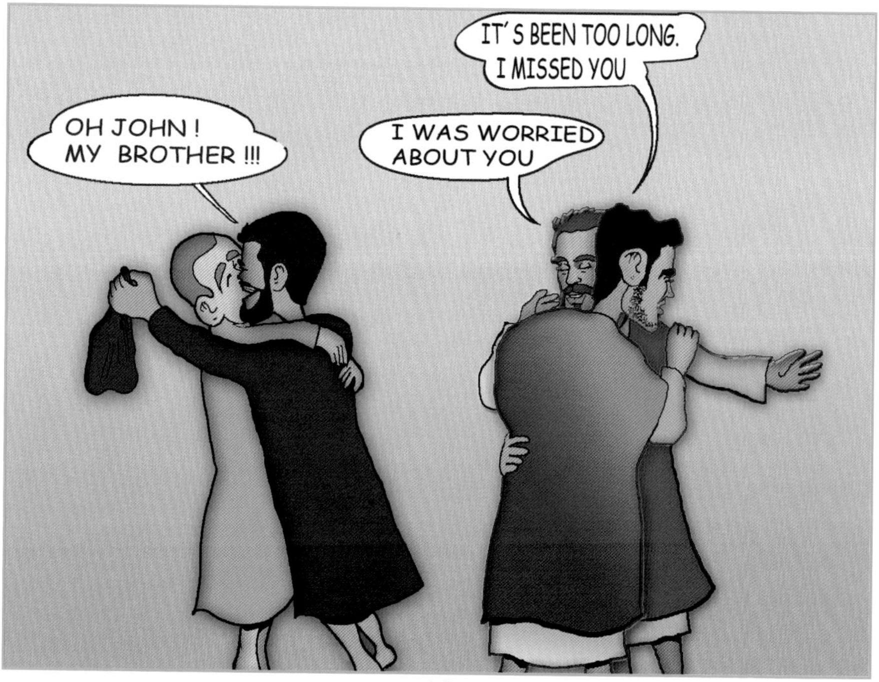
OH JOHN ! MY BROTHER !!!
I WAS WORRIED ABOUT YOU
IT' S BEEN TOO LONG. I MISSED YOU

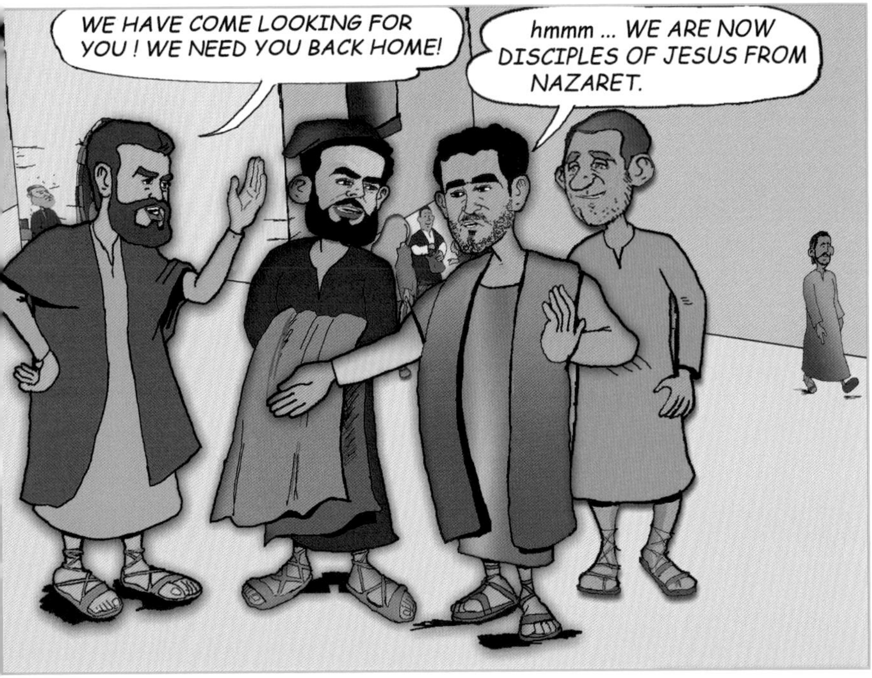
WE HAVE COME LOOKING FOR YOU ! WE NEED YOU BACK HOME!
hmmm ... WE ARE NOW DISCIPLES OF JESUS FROM NAZARET.

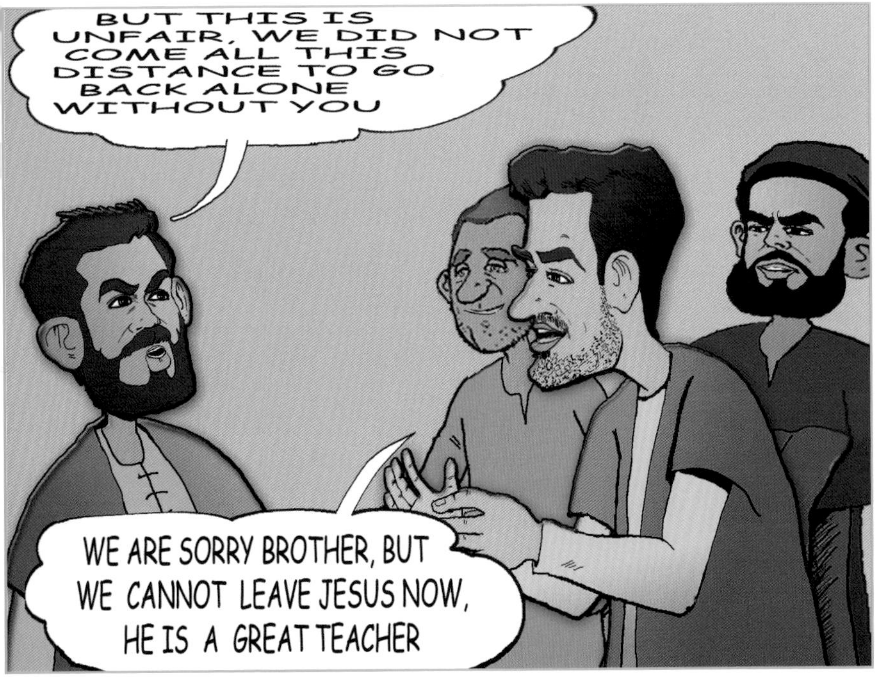
BUT THIS IS UNFAIR, WE DID NOT COME ALL THIS DISTANCE TO GO BACK ALONE WITHOUT YOU
WE ARE SORRY BROTHER, BUT WE CANNOT LEAVE JESUS NOW, HE IS A GREAT TEACHER

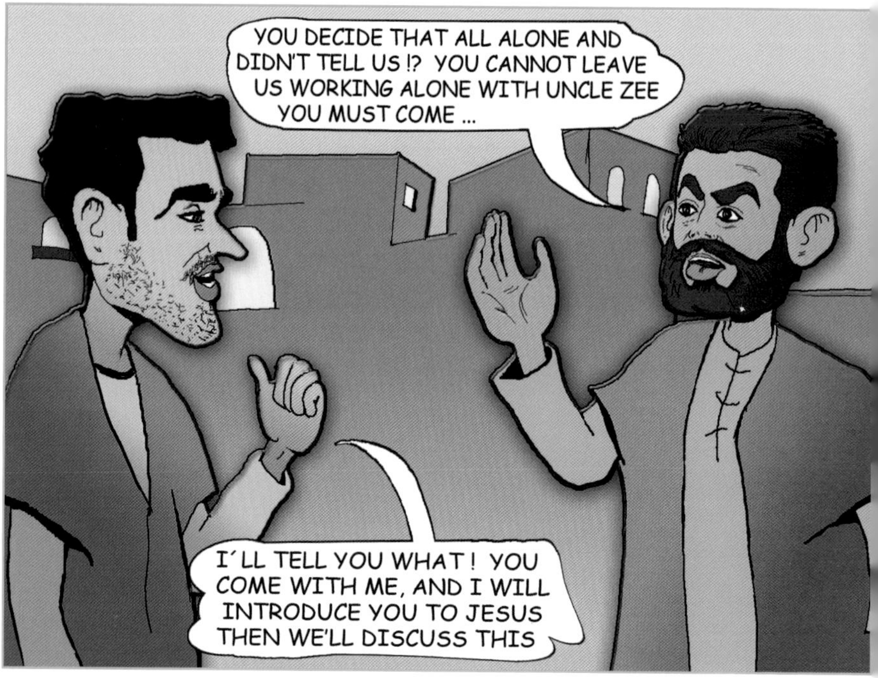
YOU DECIDE THAT ALL ALONE AND DIDN'T TELL US !? YOU CANNOT LEAVE US WORKING ALONE WITH UNCLE ZEE YOU MUST COME ...
I´LL TELL YOU WHAT ! YOU COME WITH ME, AND I WILL INTRODUCE YOU TO JESUS THEN WE'LL DISCUSS THIS

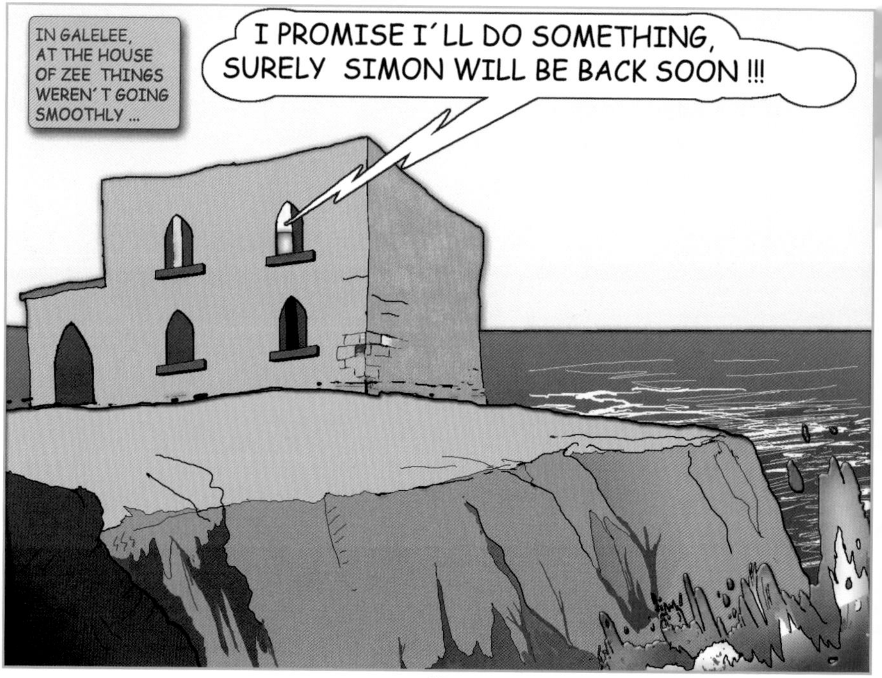
IN GALELEE, AT THE HOUSE OF ZEE THINGS WEREN´T GOING SMOOTHLY ...
I PROMISE I´LL DO SOMETHING, SURELY SIMON WILL BE BACK SOON !!!

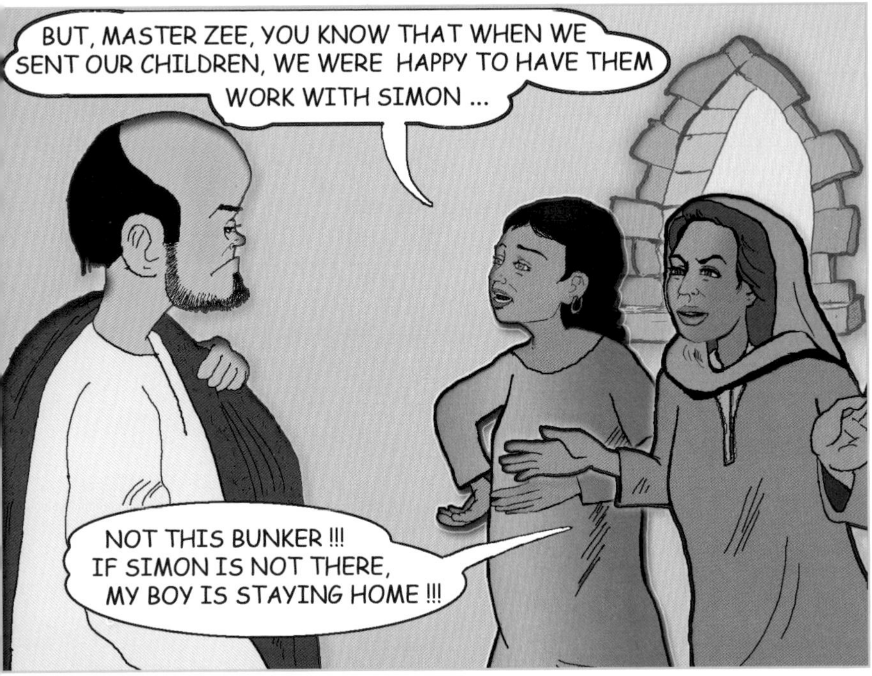
BUT, MASTER ZEE, YOU KNOW THAT WHEN WE SENT OUR CHILDREN, WE WERE HAPPY TO HAVE THEM WORK WITH SIMON ...
NOT THIS BUNKER !!! IF SIMON IS NOT THERE, MY BOY IS STAYING HOME !!!

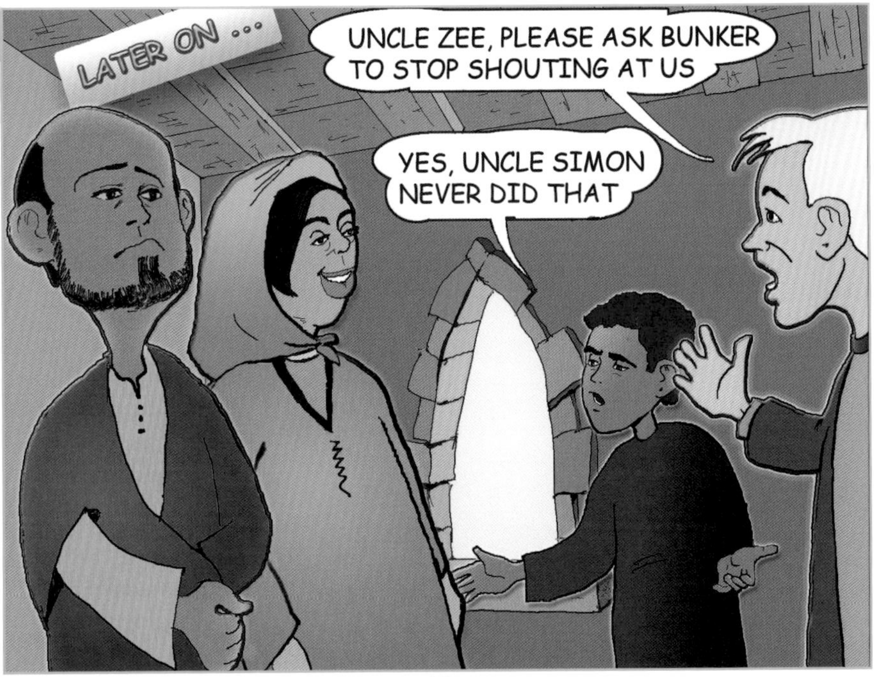
LATER ON ...
UNCLE ZEE, PLEASE ASK BUNKER TO STOP SHOUTING AT US
YES, UNCLE SIMON NEVER DID THAT

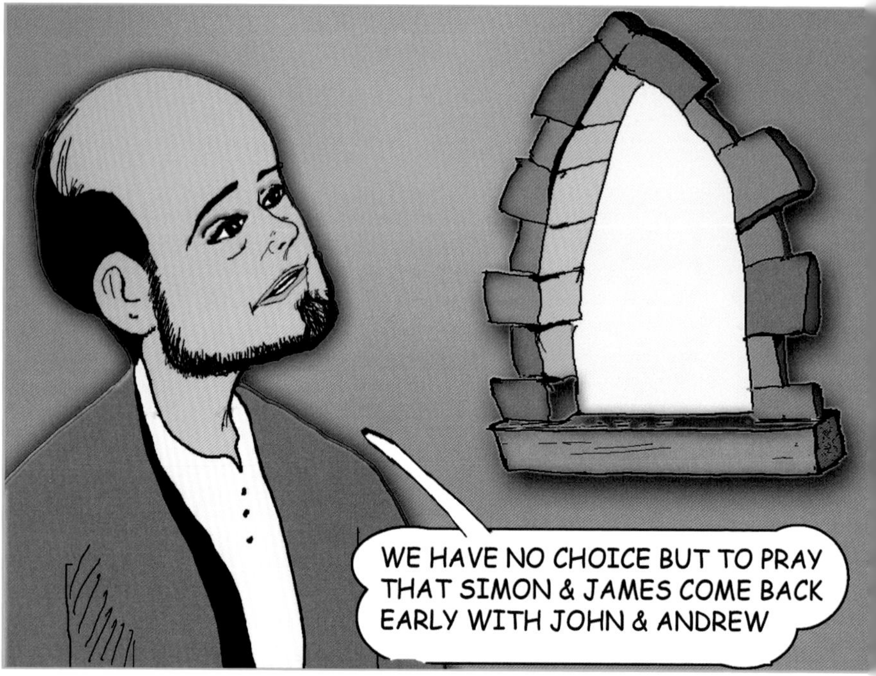
WE HAVE NO CHOICE BUT TO PRAY THAT SIMON & JAMES COME BACK EARLY WITH JOHN & ANDREW

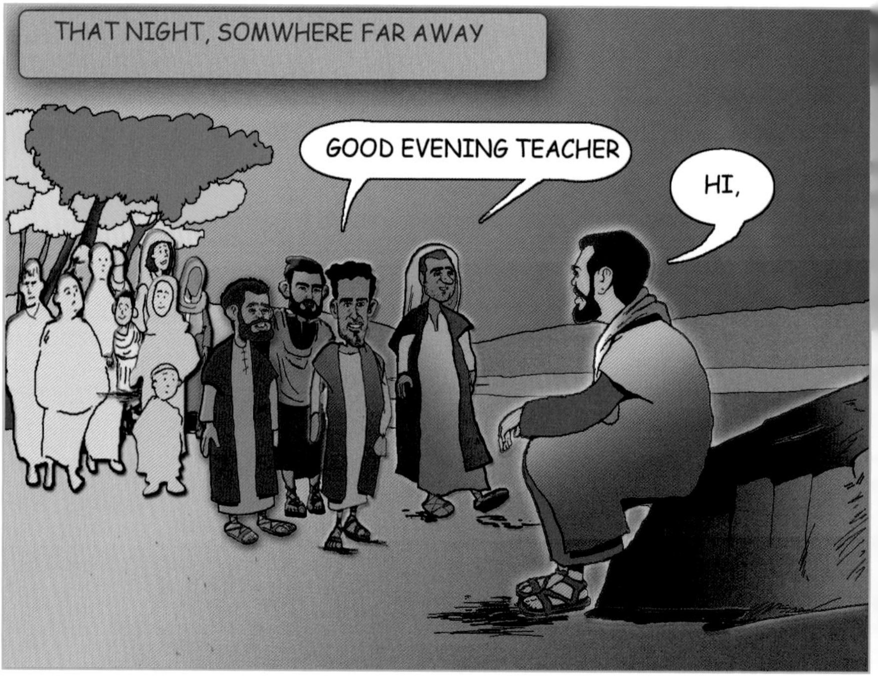
THAT NIGHT, SOMWHERE FAR AWAY
GOOD EVENING TEACHER
HI,

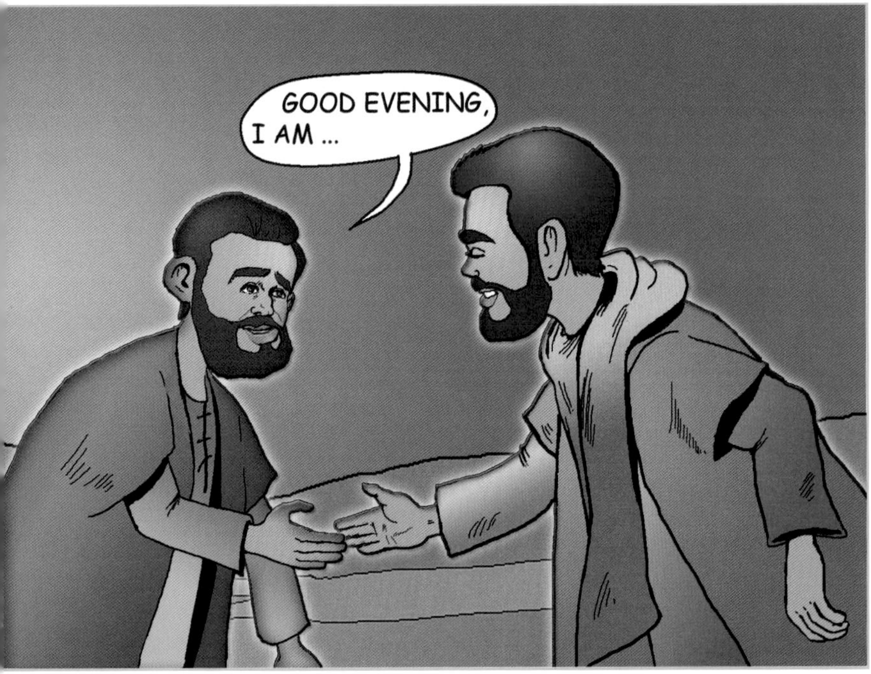
GOOD EVENING, I AM ...

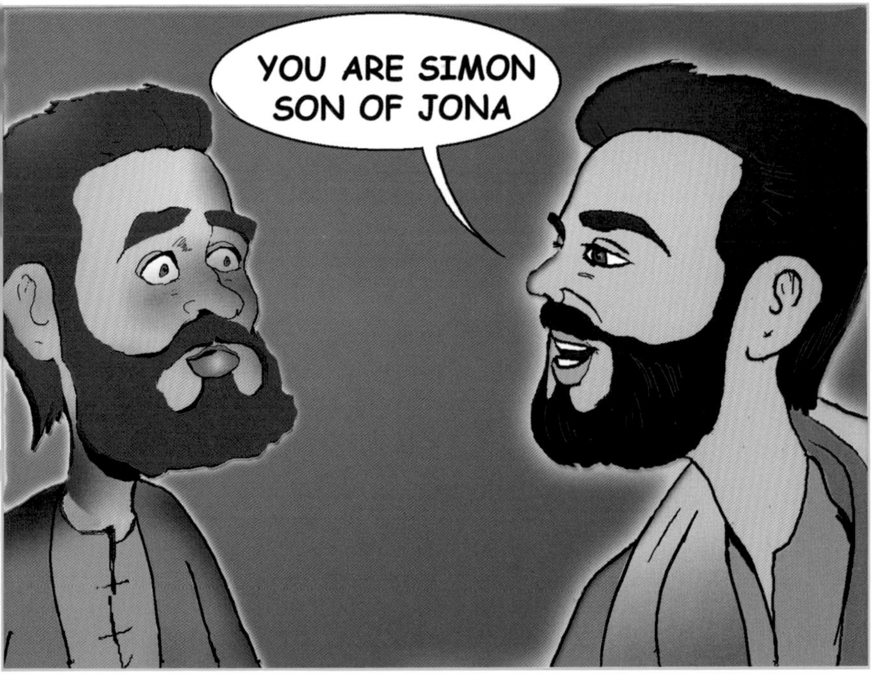
YOU ARE SIMON SON OF JONA

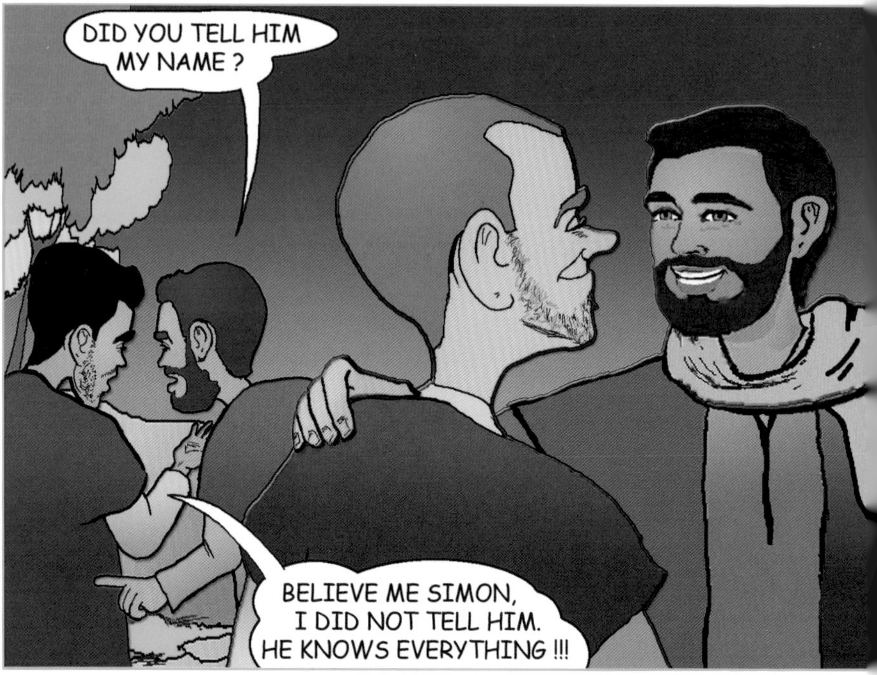
DID YOU TELL HIM MY NAME ?
BELIEVE ME SIMON, I DID NOT TELL HIM. HE KNOWS EVERYTHING !!!

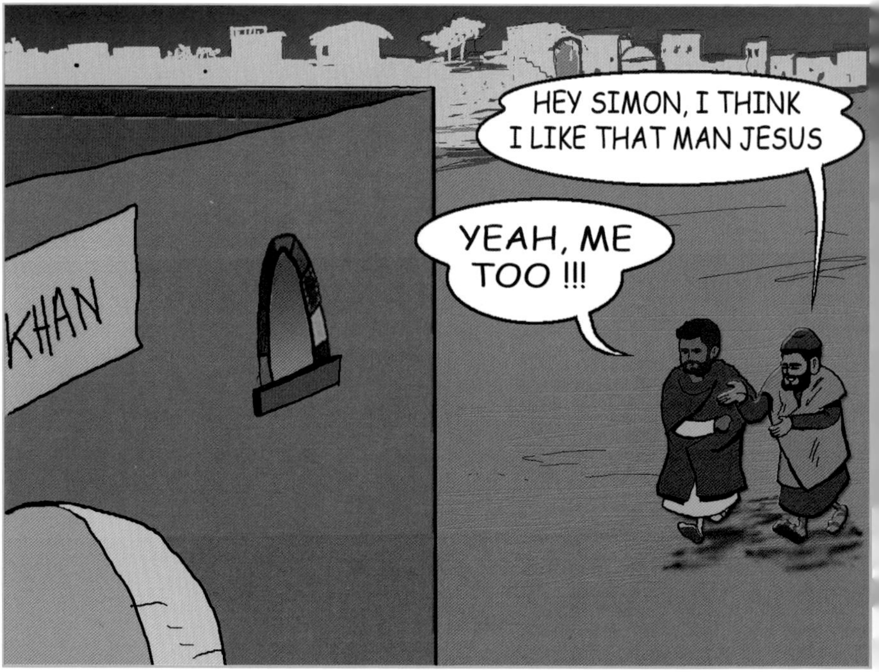
HEY SIMON, I THINK I LIKE THAT MAN JESUS
YEAH, ME TOO !!!
KHAN

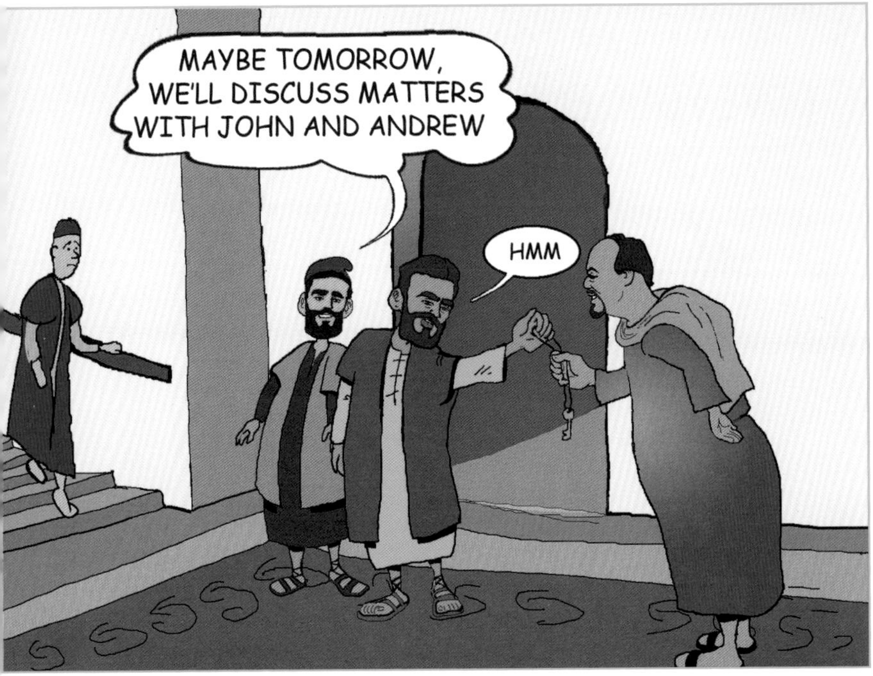
MAYBE TOMORROW, WE'LL DISCUSS MATTERS WITH JOHN AND ANDREW
HMM

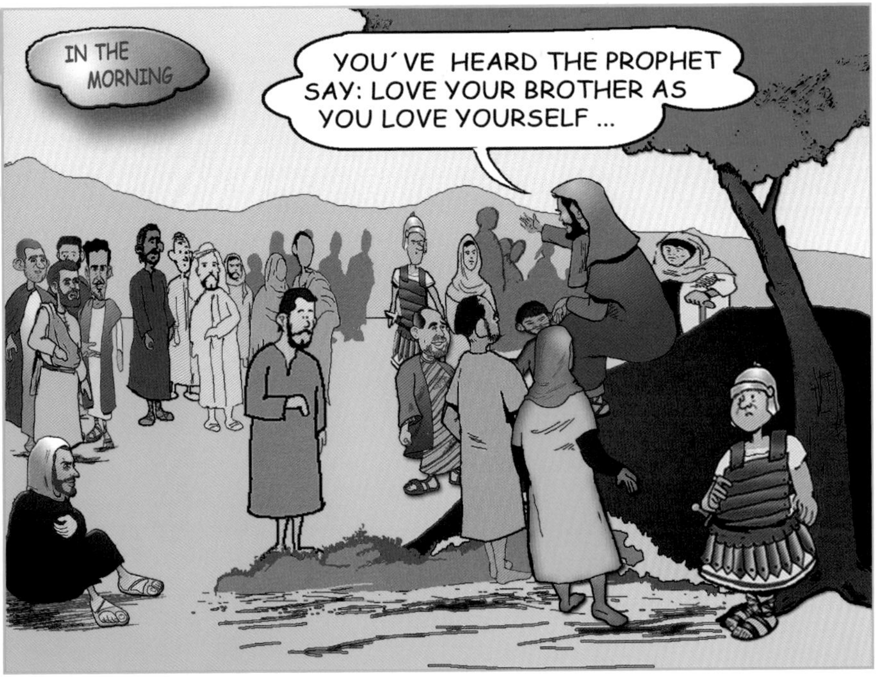
IN THE MORNING
YOU´VE HEARD THE PROPHET SAY: LOVE YOUR BROTHER AS YOU LOVE YOURSELF ...

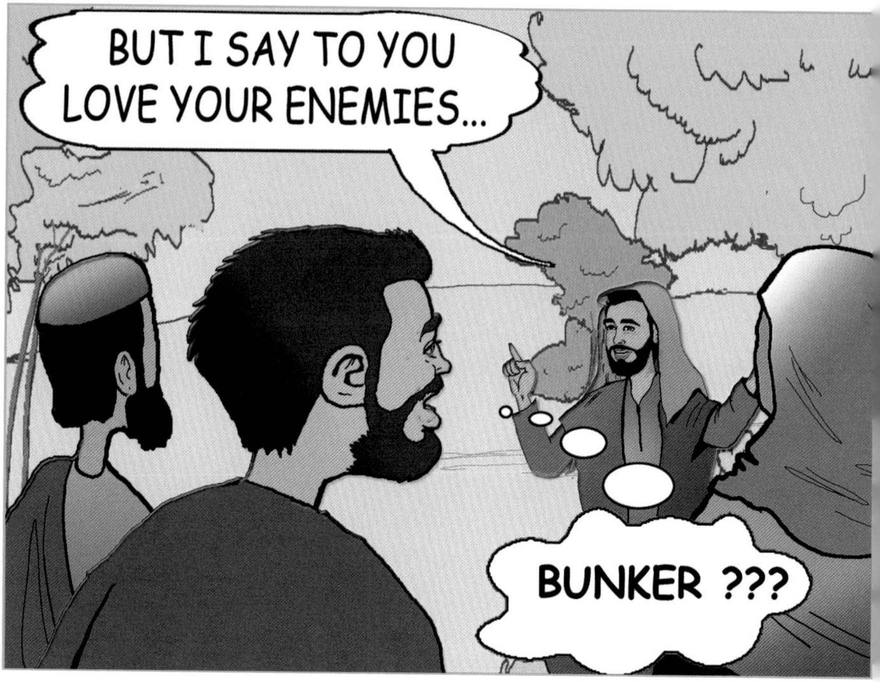
BUT I SAY TO YOU LOVE YOUR ENEMIES...
BUNKER ???

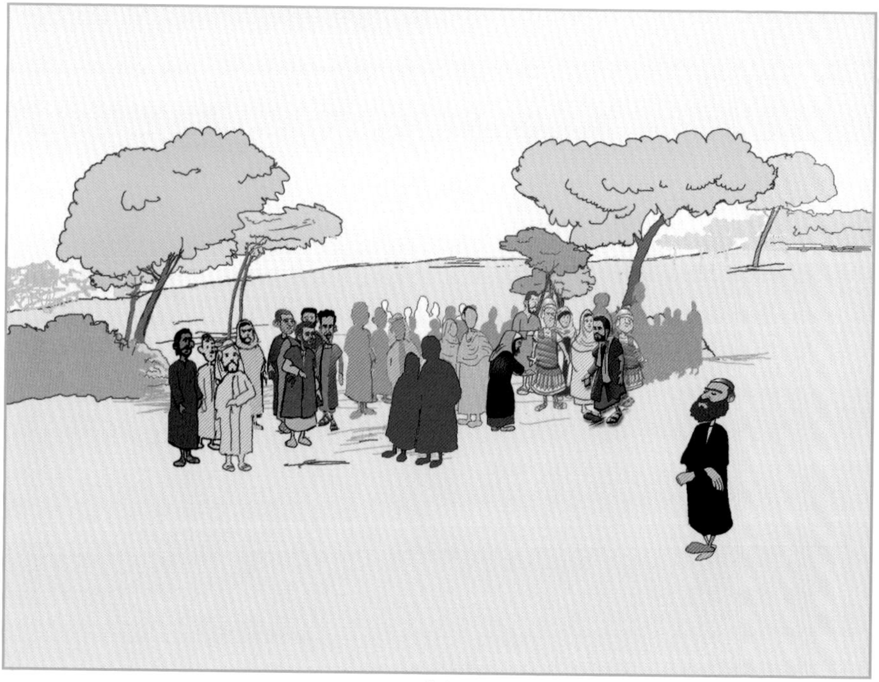

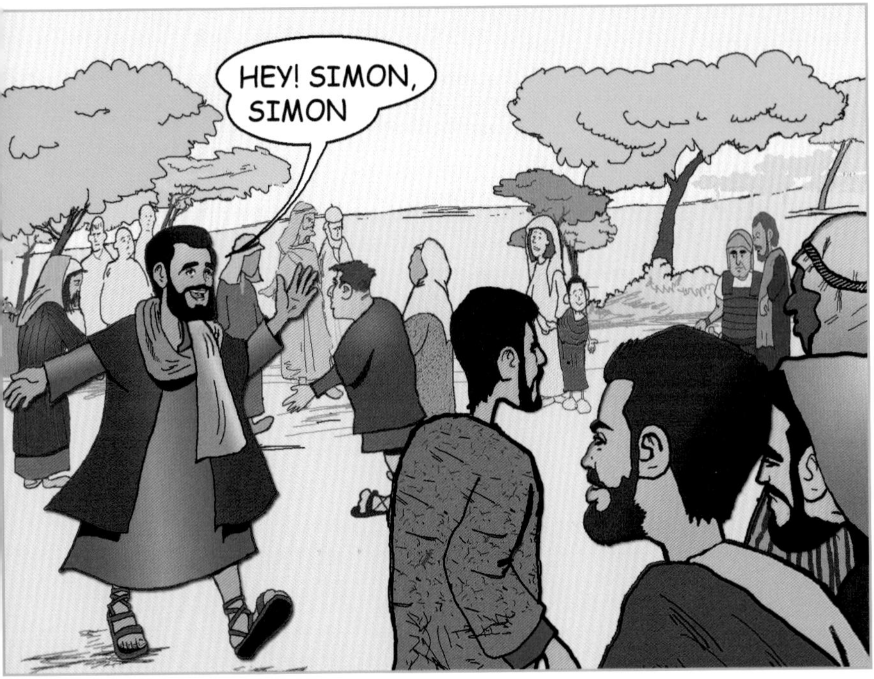
HEY! SIMON, SIMON

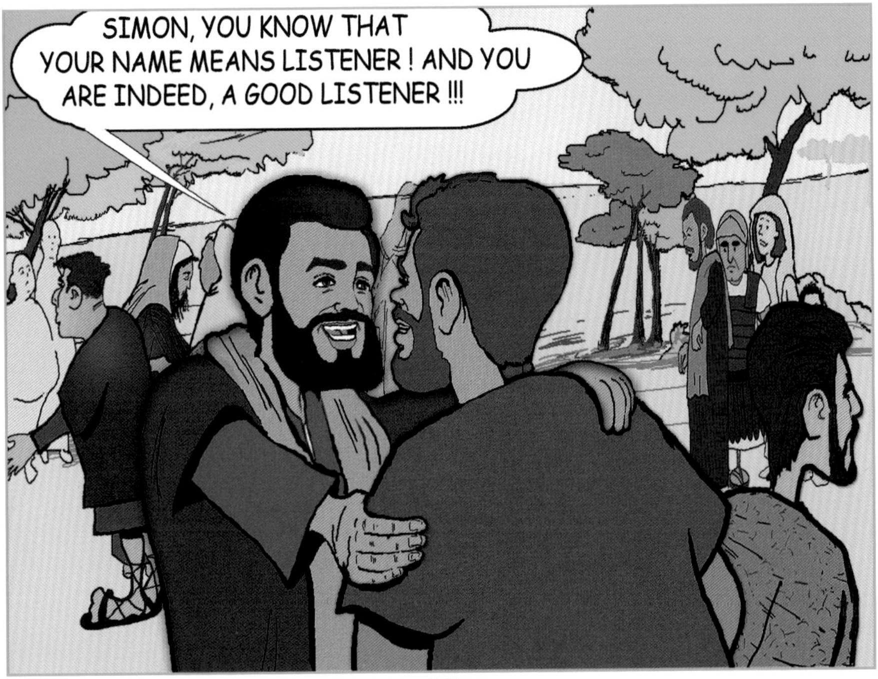
SIMON, YOU KNOW THAT YOUR NAME MEANS LISTENER ! AND YOU ARE INDEED, A GOOD LISTENER !!!

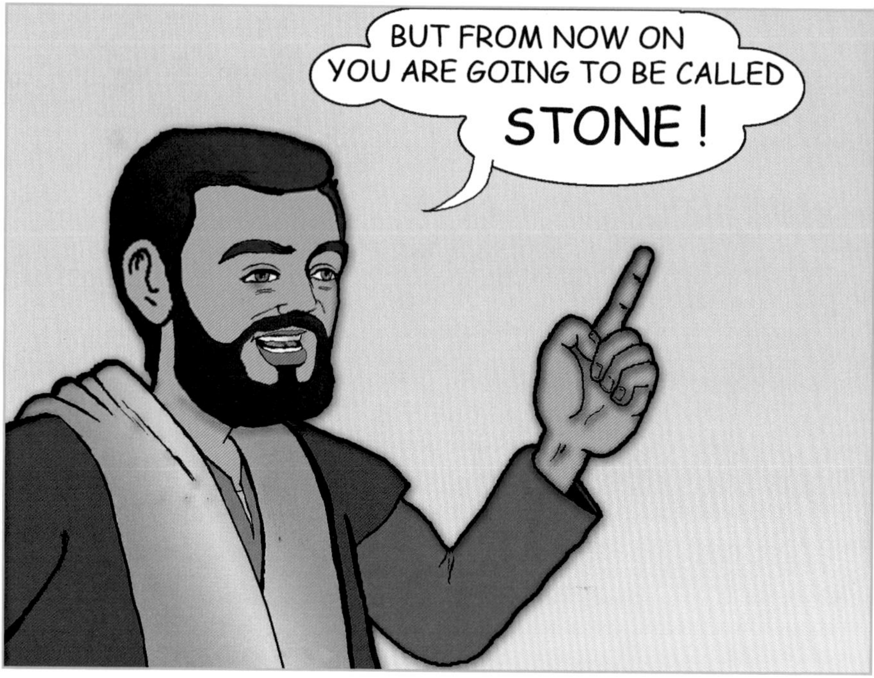
BUT FROM NOW ON YOU ARE GOING TO BE CALLED STONE !

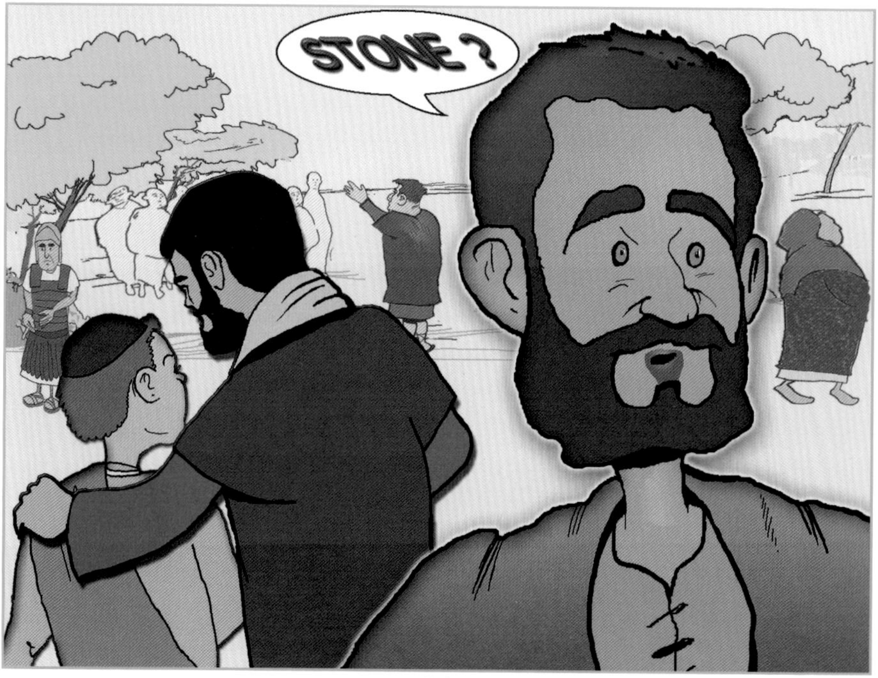
STONE ?

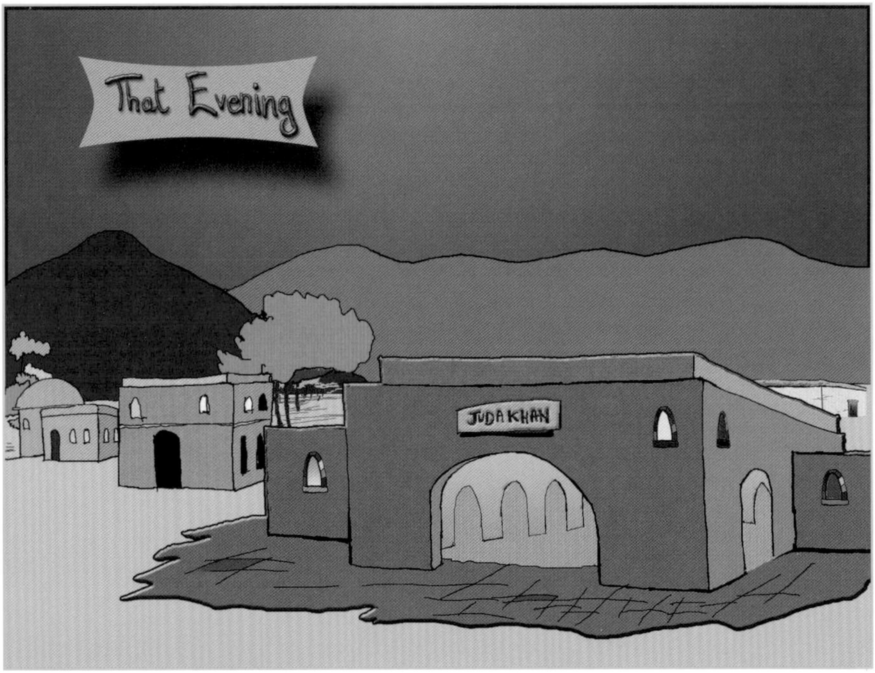
That Evening
JUDAKHAN

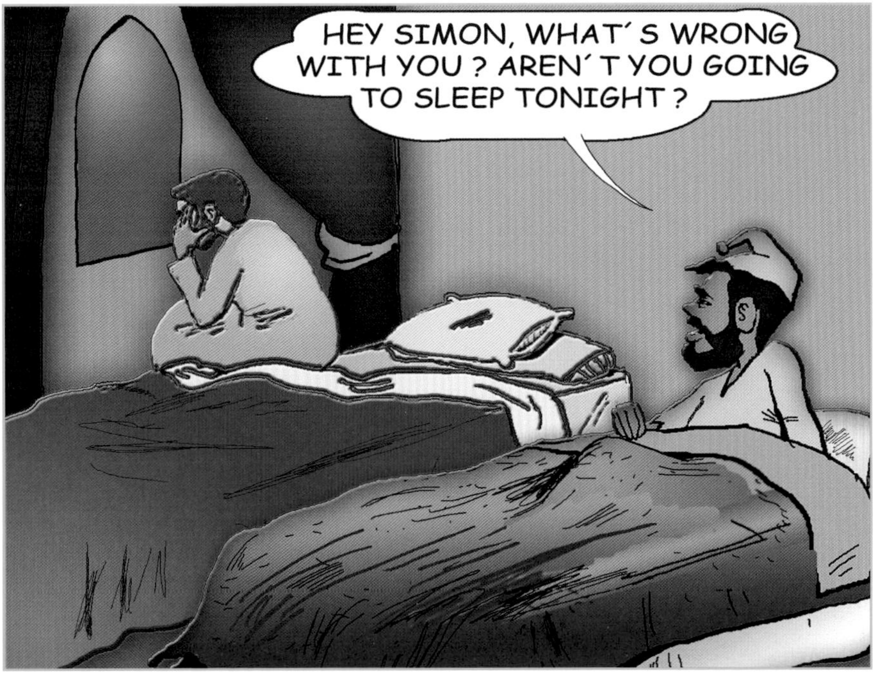
HEY SIMON, WHAT´S WRONG WITH YOU ? AREN´T YOU GOING TO SLEEP TONIGHT ?

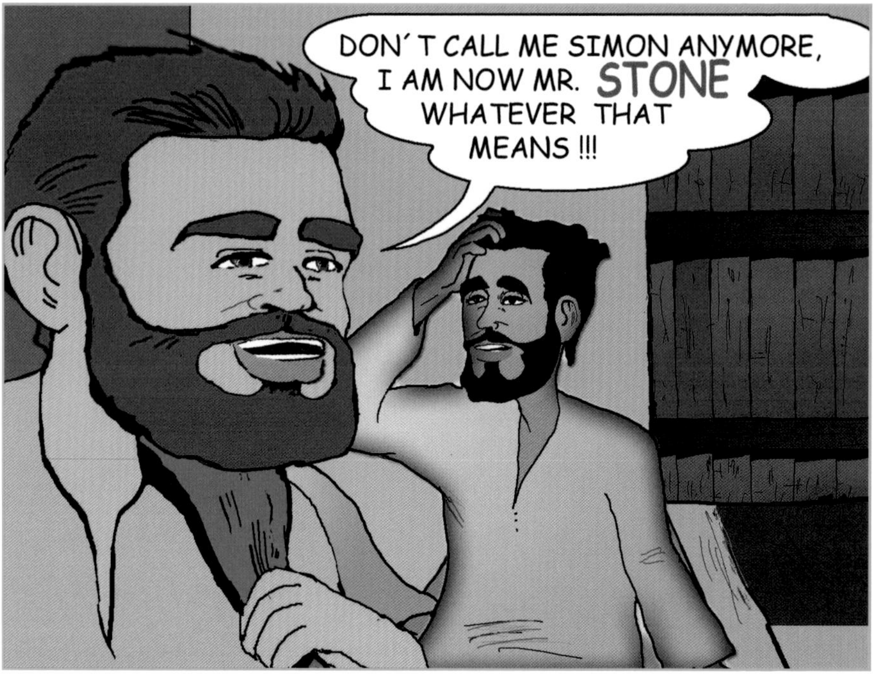
DON´T CALL ME SIMON ANYMORE, I AM NOW MR. STONE WHATEVER THAT MEANS !!!

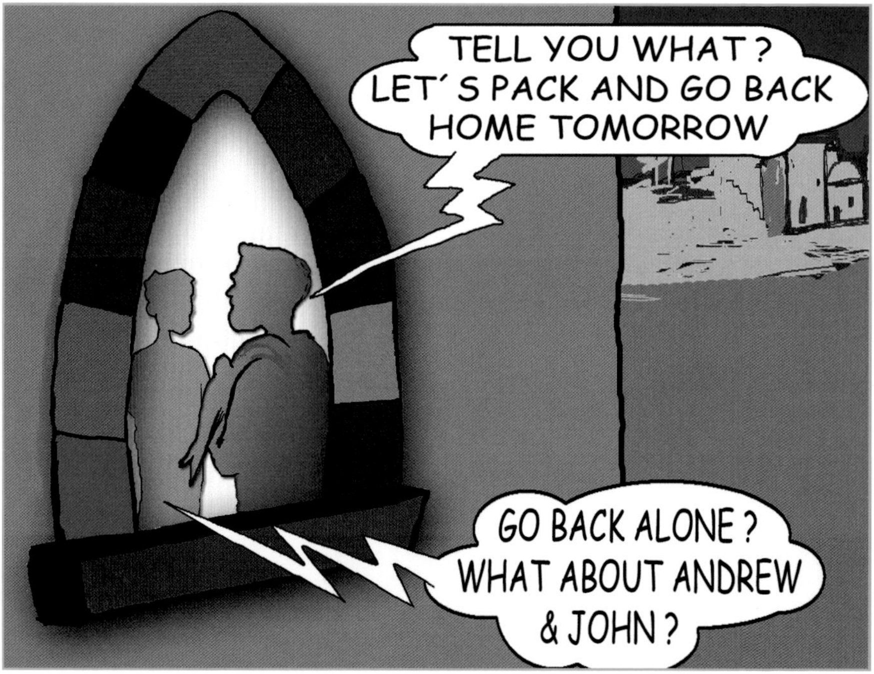
TELL YOU WHAT ? LET´S PACK AND GO BACK HOME TOMORROW
GO BACK ALONE ? WHAT ABOUT ANDREW & JOHN ?

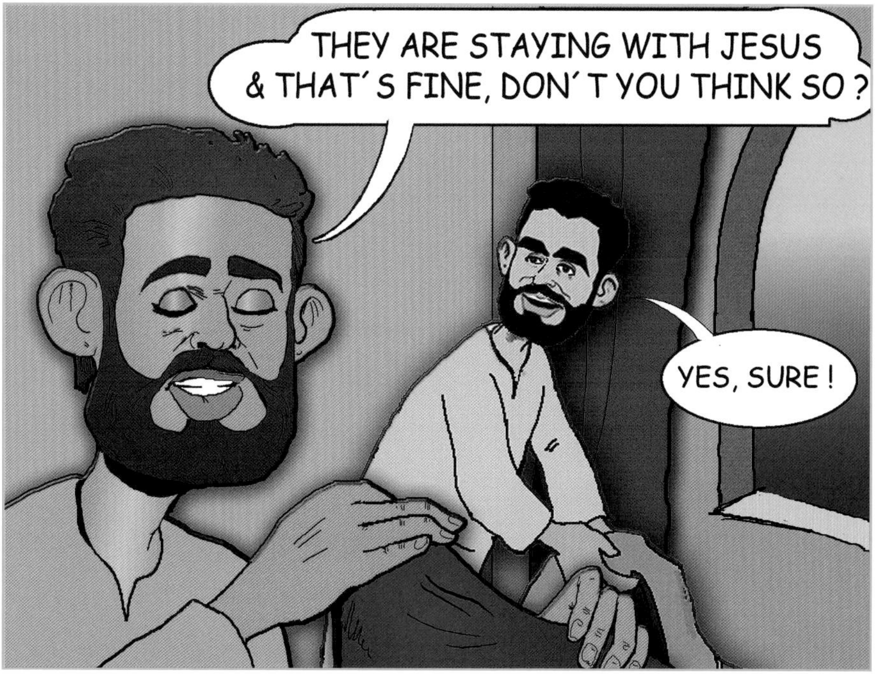
THEY ARE STAYING WITH JESUS & THAT´S FINE, DON´T YOU THINK SO ?
YES, SURE !

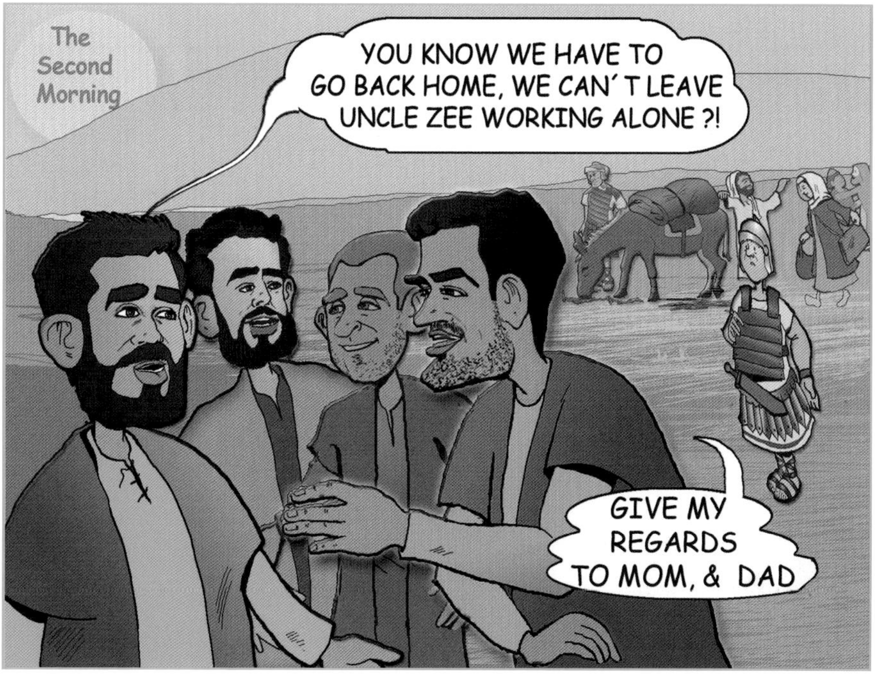
The Second Morning
YOU KNOW WE HAVE TO GO BACK HOME, WE CAN´T LEAVE UNCLE ZEE WORKING ALONE ?!
GIVE MY REGARDS TO MOM, & DAD

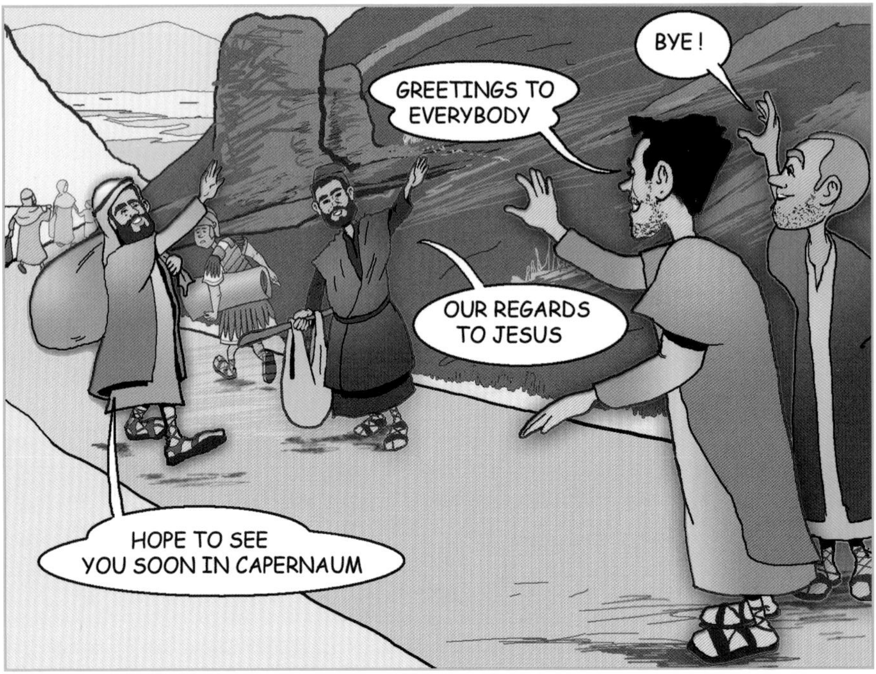
BYE !
GREETINGS TO EVERYBODY
OUR REGARDS TO JESUS
HOPE TO SEE YOU SOON IN CAPERNAUM

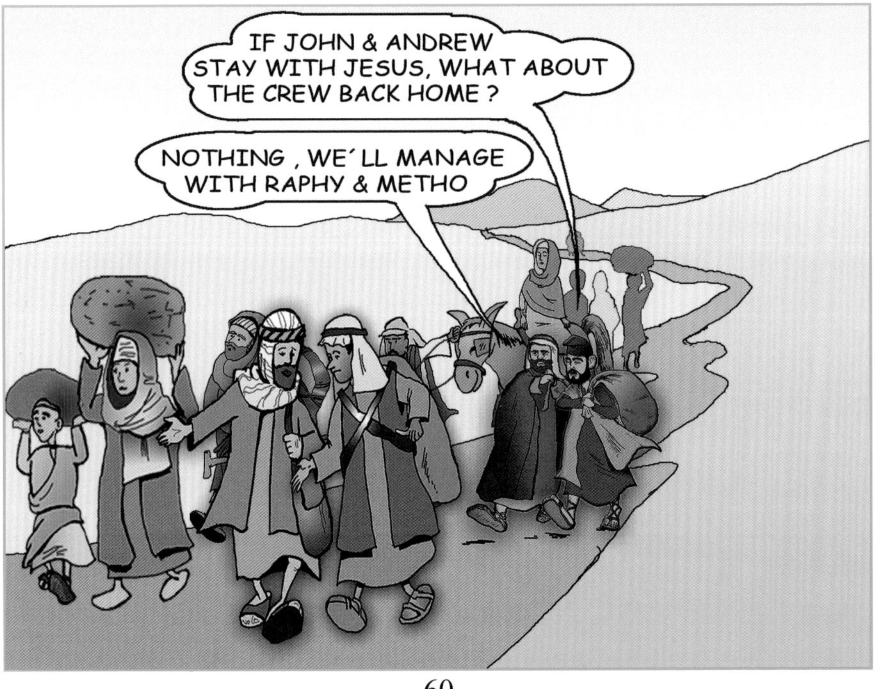
IF JOHN & ANDREW STAY WITH JESUS, WHAT ABOUT THE CREW BACK HOME ?
NOTHING , WE´LL MANAGE WITH RAPHY & METHO

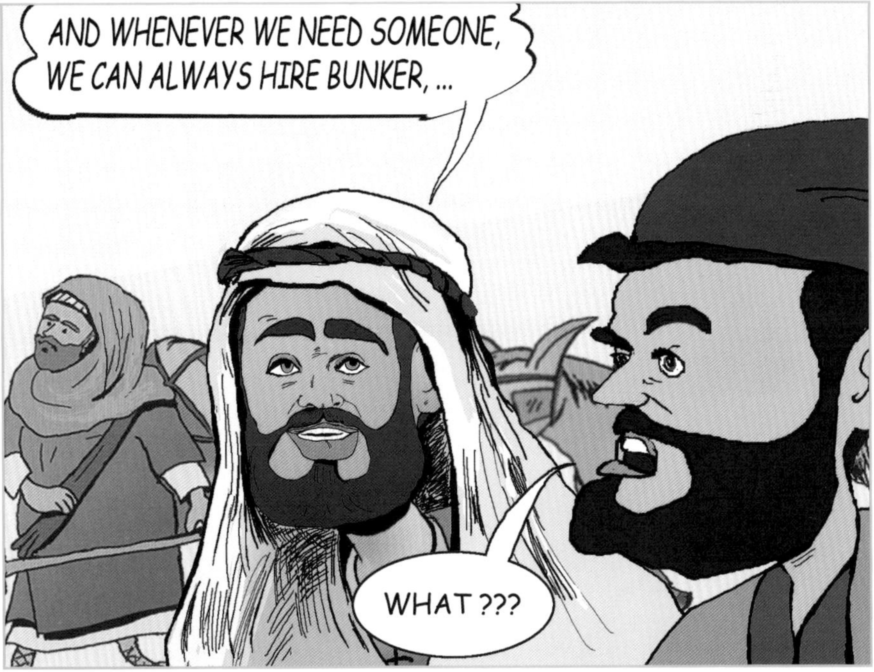
AND WHENEVER WE NEED SOMEONE, WE CAN ALWAYS HIRE BUNKER, ...
WHAT ???

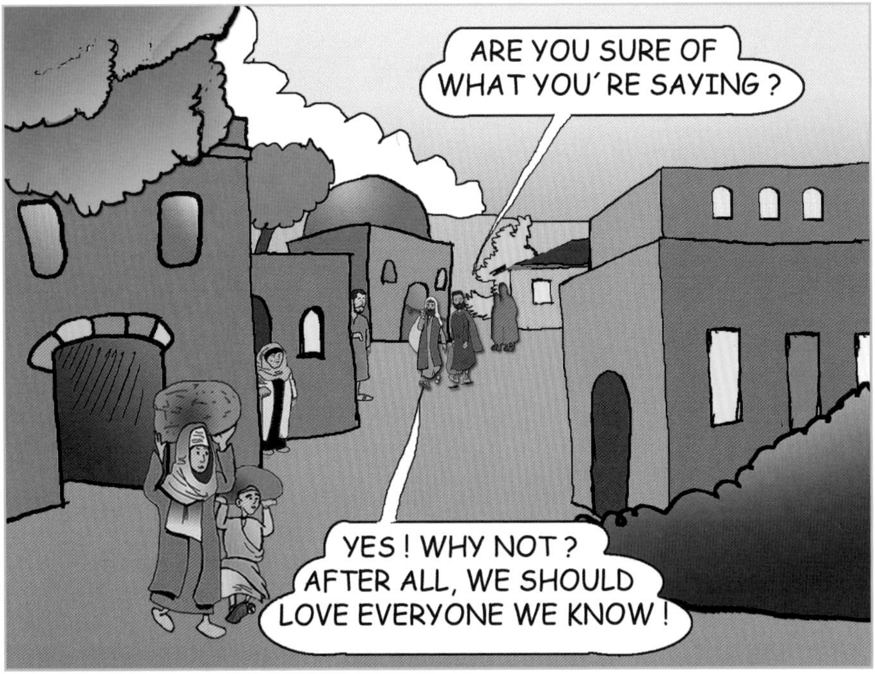
ARE YOU SURE OF WHAT YOU´RE SAYING ?
YES ! WHY NOT ? AFTER ALL, WE SHOULD LOVE EVERYONE WE KNOW !

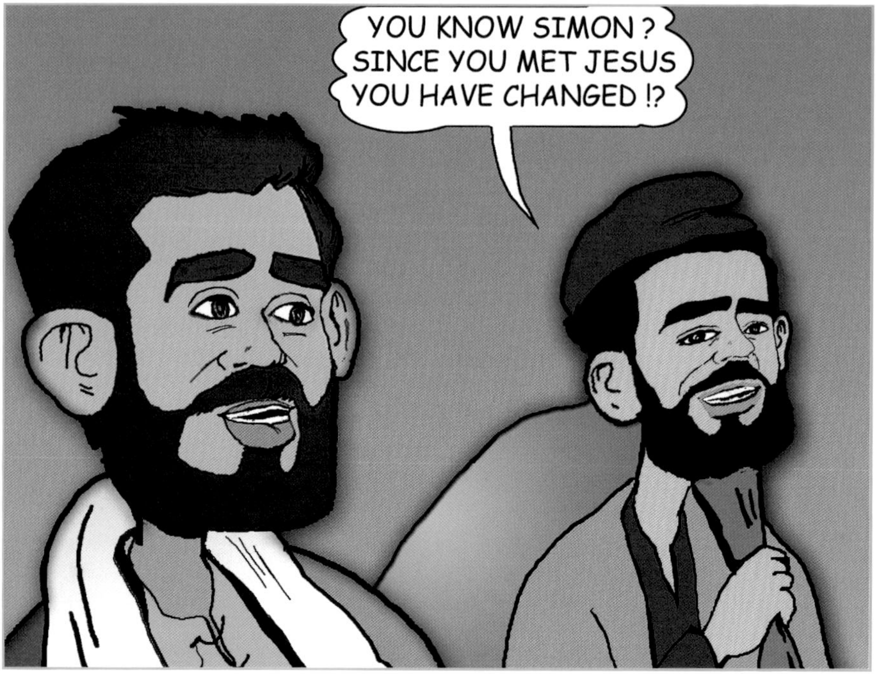
YOU KNOW SIMON ? SINCE YOU MET JESUS YOU HAVE CHANGED !?

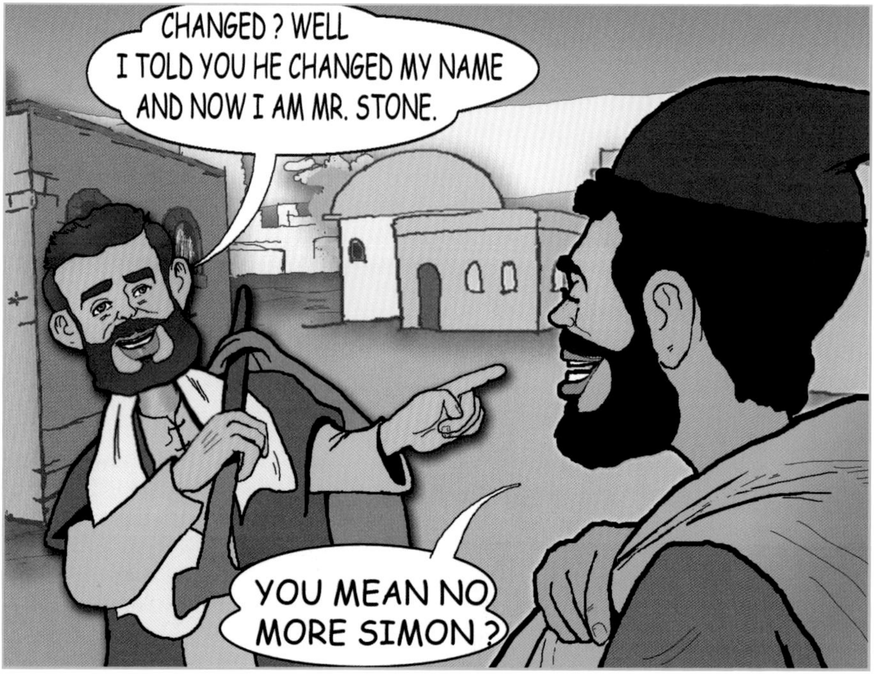
CHANGED ? WELL I TOLD YOU HE CHANGED MY NAME AND NOW I AM MR. STONE.
YOU MEAN NO MORE SIMON ?

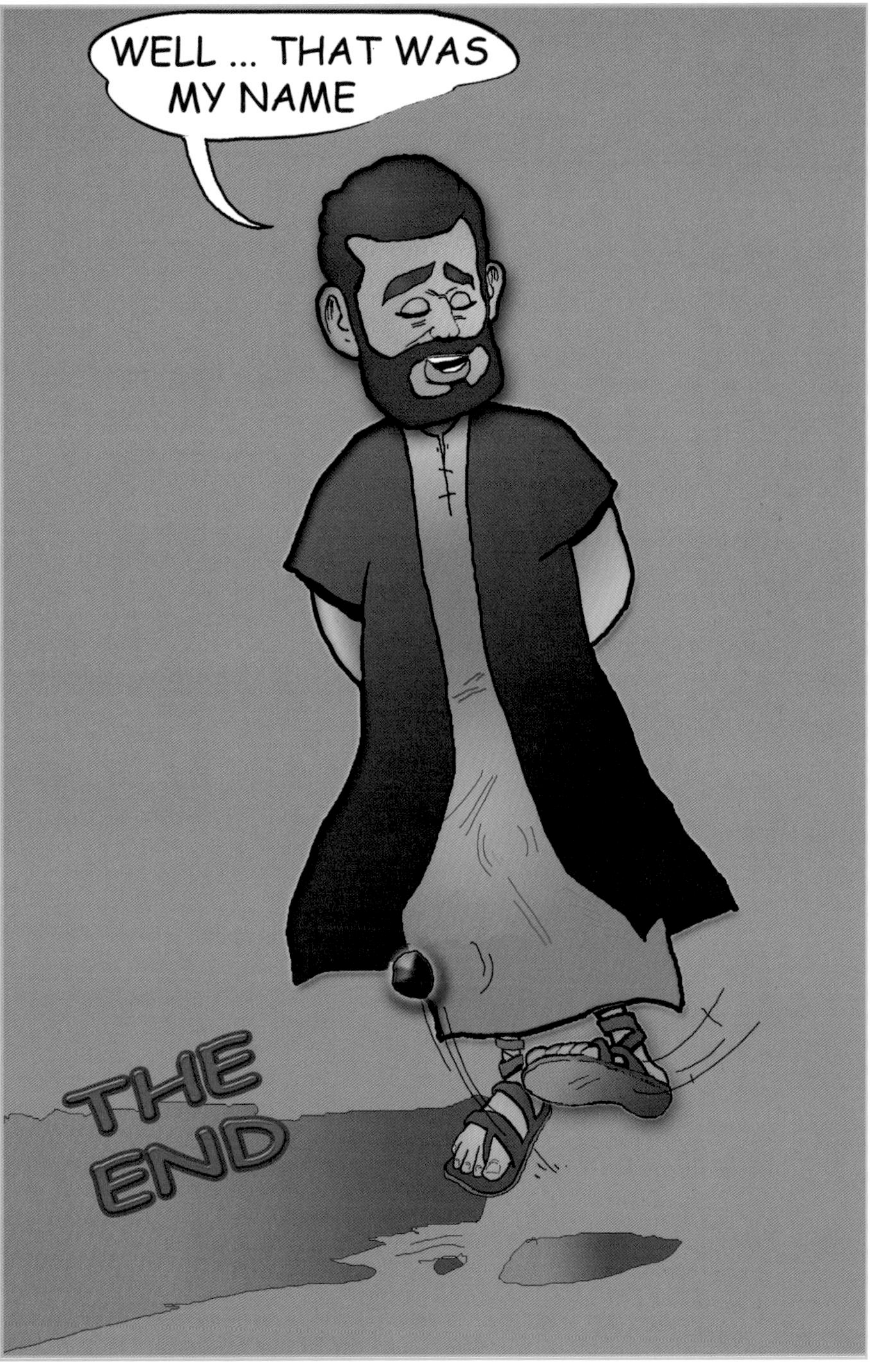
WELL ... THAT WAS MY NAME
THE END

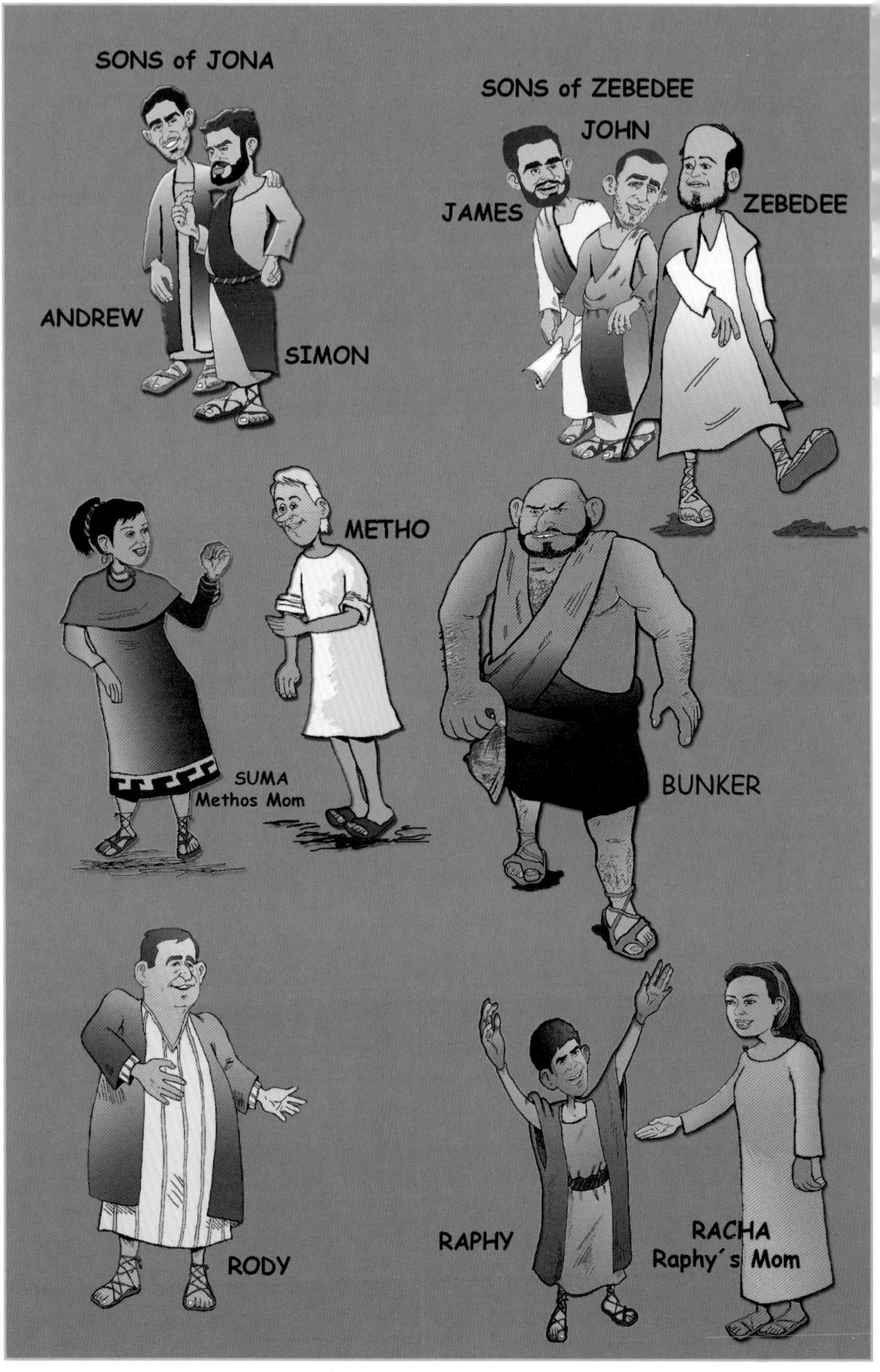
SONS of JONA
ANDREW
SIMON
SONS of ZEBEDEE
JOHN
JAMES
ZEBEDEE
METHO
SUMA
Methos Mom
BUNKER
RODY
RAPHY
RACHA
Raphy´s Mom